Southwest Philly

by

Harvey Pitts

DEDICATION

This writing is dedicated to my best friend and the love of my life, my wife Mary. Without her encouragement and positive critique, this writing could have never been finished.

And also who without the technical assistance of my niece Reneé Hansell Langford, I could never have put it all together. She really is great.

Thank you to both.

Table of Contents

CHAPTER 15

CHAPTER 16

FOREWORD

IT WAS IN THE YEAR 2011 that I started writing this story. I was almost sixty-five years old.

After reading the first chapter of this book, I felt it was necessary to write this foreword because the beginning sounds so sad, and honestly, my life has been nothing less than joyful and full, even though it started out rather poorly. Should anyone honor me and read this, I hope my life can serve as an example that you can change the direction of your life through hard work and a little divine intervention. I will mention my spiritual beliefs now because, unfortunately, lots of people get turned off when you speak of God. If you have problems with God, please read on. I promise not to bore you. Perhaps after reading this, you may gain a little faith.

I got the idea to write this from my mentor, Bert Actman. I understand from Bert, it took years for him to write his own story. After Bert read my first chapter, he told me I needed help. He offered to be my ghost-writer, and I gladly accepted his offer. This worked very well until July 2013, when Bert (pictured right) passed away. I truly miss his friendship, advice, and wisdom in this writing, as well as in my life. I didn't think I would ever say that heaven would be a better place, but I'm sure it is with Bert there. God bless his memory and soul.

I also had help from the program Dragon, which is a voice-recognition program. This is a great program. I talk, it types. You see, I rank up there with the world's worst spellers. Because of my inability to spell, I can take a book like War and Peace and reduce it to a paragraph. I spend so much time checking my spelling, and using other words I do know how to spell, that it takes me forever to write something. With this program, I don't have to worry about it. If you learn one thing, please learn to spell and the proper use of grammar. The only way I graduated from high school was by taking the weirdo courses like mass-media film study and public speaking. When it came to grammar, I had to cheat.

There are many people and events in my life that I did not mention in this book, unfortunately. They are not mentioned, but they are still important to me.

Some names have been changed to protect the privacy of individuals and companies. It's not my intention to harm anyone.

CHAPTER 1

Southwest Philly

Haverford Avenue

MY NAME IS HARVEY PITTS. I was born on February 2, 1947, Groundhog Day. I don't know if the groundhog saw his shadow. When I was born, there was a blizzard. The vehicle my mom was riding in couldn't go any farther, so in a house next to a rag shop (in the 1940s, you could gather all your rags and take them to a shop where they would buy them by the pound) is where I was born on Fallon Street in West Philadelphia. The following day they took me to Presbyterian Hospital, where they predicted that I would not survive because I was two months premature. They were wrong.

My oldest memory is walking across 34th Street and Haverford Avenue at the age of two or three, hand in hand with my mother, Ruth Roberta Harvey Pitts, tiptoeing through the horse shit left by the iceman, milkman, bread man, and the fruit and vegetable huckster. For you see, in 1949 most of the vehicles delivering in our neighborhood were horse-drawn wagons. Motor vehicles were still not that affordable.

We lived at 3415 Haverford Avenue over the butcher shop right across the street from the firehouse, Engine 44 built in 1908, at 3420 Haverford Avenue.

We lived in a one-bedroom, one-room hellhole. My mom was probably thirty-eight years old, my brother Jackie was four or five, I was two or three, and Donny

had just been born. I remember Donny (left) coming home from the hospital with my mom. He was the cutest little baby that anyone had ever seen, with little curls in his hair. Everyone just loved him. Up to that point, they used to love me. I was a little jealous.

We lived in this horrible building because my mother was constantly trying to hide from my father. My father was an alcoholic merchant marine. Every time he came home, he beat my mother, just because he liked to beat women. Thank God he didn't come home often. It seemed she had black eyes all the time, and was always explaining to everyone that she was just downright clumsy. No one walked into that many things.

My mother forced Jackie, Donny, and me to go to Sunday school. I think the church was helping us. Even then we were on welfare. I don't think my father gave her anything. In those days welfare was not what it is today. It was something to be ashamed of. People came and inspected our home. We could not even have life

insurance, and my mother constantly said that we would be buried in the potter's field if we died. So, in secret, Mom purchased life insurance policies so that we would not be buried in the potter's field. These policies came in very handy in our move to Levittown, Pennsylvania, later on.

Any old memories of Haverford Avenue would have to include Miss Becky, and that's what we called her: Miss Becky. She was truly a nice person. She was the only other white person in the neighborhood (her house is pictured right). She would send Jackie to the corner for her groceries, and she would give him a nickel, which was a lot of money. As I got older, I would go to the corner for her groceries. When I say "older," I was five and Jackie was about seven.

I mentioned earlier that we once lived across the street from a firehouse. This firehouse was an old-fashioned type, with a Dalmatian dog and a slide pole from

the second floor. The firemen in this firehouse used to make their own meals, and if they made too much or if they had a fire to fight, they would give Mom the leftovers. Jackie and I at times would lock Mom out of the apartment, and the firemen would have to stop traffic on Haverford Avenue and send their ladder from the ladder truck up to our window. Jackie and I thought it was the coolest thing in the world. I guess you understand that my mother didn't think it was so cool, and Jackie and I paid dearly.

When we got a little older, Mom would let us play in the neighborhood. This opened a new world for us. We could go to the zoo, which was only about four blocks away. There was a hole in the fence near the railroad track, which we used for admission. We also could go swimming in our underpants in the fountains at the Philadelphia

Museum of Art (above), or climb down the hills next to the art museum to get to the aquarium (right).

During the time we lived on Haverford Avenue, I attended school at Morton McMichael Elementary School at 35th and Fairmount Avenue. Jackie and I were the only white

students in the school. In first grade I liked Sherry. She was a beautiful little black girl. Unfortunately, Sherry didn't like me. I didn't care at the time. I thought white people were the minority.

We were poor, but really didn't know how poor we were. My grandfather Bill Harvey (known as Grandpop Harvey) and my Aunt Mary and cousin Patsy lived at 48th and Brown Street. Mom would put Jackie (pictured right), Donny, and

me (pictured left) in a wagon or sled when the snow was on the ground and pull us to Aunt Mary's, where we would eat. Quite often Aunt Mary, Grandpop, and Patsy ate hamburgers while Mom, my brothers, and I ate diluted soup. I guess something beats nothing. We were grateful for the food. They also had a television; as you can guess, we didn't. I loved Patsy and so did Jackie. She would sneak us things at times, namely goodies. However, to watch television or to get the goodies, we had

to turn rope for her or, and this is somewhat disgusting, she loved to pick our scabs. Jackie and I would be bleeding all over everything, and Aunt Mary would beat the hell out of us for getting blood all over, but we had goodies while we watched television. It was worth it. My Aunt Mary liked to bake cakes. She could cut cake so thin you could see through it. When she was baking cakes, Jackie and I would run around the house stomping our feet on the floor, doing everything to make sure the cake did not rise. Of course, we would get beaten with the towel bar, but we got to eat the whole cake. One of the last things I recall about Haverford Avenue is when I got circumcised at age five. Unfortunately, the hospital never bothered to perform this procedure at birth, because of my life expectancy, and at that time we were on welfare and the welfare department would've had to pay. We lived at 34th and Haverford Avenue, and the hospital was at 40th and Market Street. After the operation Mom and I had to walk home since she had no money for a cab and the wagon was broken. I will never forget the terrific pain in my groin.

Baring Street

FROM HAVERFORD AVENUE, WE MOVED to Baring Street. This was more of a shit hole than where we used to live. I believe there was a slumlord who owned this property. The cockroaches owned the kitchen and bathroom. The only memories I have, other than the cockroaches, are that our babysitters sexually abused  Jackie and me. These girls were real white trash. I have no idea where Mom found them. We didn't live there very long, maybe six or seven months.

Belmont Avenue

WE NEXT MOVED TO THE corner of Belmont and Girard Avenues, which was, ironically, across the street from another firehouse that also had a Dalmatian. We never developed a relationship with the firemen. This move brought us closer to Grandpop's, and also to my sister Sophia's apartment, which was on Lancaster Avenue. My sister Sophia became and remained one of the closest women in my life, only outdone by my wife Mary and my mother. My mom would then either take us to Grandpop's or Sophia's, where we always could find a meal. My sister Sophia was married to Walter Parkhurst. They appeared to be a great couple. My sister, when I was born, asked my mother if she could raise me as her son. Sophia is nineteen years older than I am. My mother said no. Sophia has always had a special place in my heart. She and Walter were Santa and Mrs. Claus when we were younger. If the weather was bad or if they had trouble with the '52 Ford, Santa Claus would be late.

Sophia and Walt would also pick us up for their vacation to Wildwood, New Jersey. We would all stay at Aunt Mary's, for Grandpop had died and she inherited everything. During our stay at Wildwood, Jackie, Donny, and I would sleep in the attic. It was really hot, but we were at the shore. Some memorable things about Wildwood were that Jackie, first, and then I got jobs at the bowling alley. Another was the time the police came to Aunt Mary's. Jackie or I had bought a knife that was too big, and it caused all kinds of problems. Aunt Mary would make us onion or sugar sandwiches, and made sure we ate every bit of it. The onion sandwiches sucked. Once cousin Patsy and Jackie hung me on the clothesline. Last but not least, Jackie and I would get blisters from the sun, and Patsy would insist on breaking the blisters. Jackie and I got to watch television and get goodies as a reward for allowing her to cause that much pain.

I believe my mother, Jackie, Donny, and I were excluded from the will because my grandfather never accepted us as his grandchildren. He never did anything for us, other than feed us soup at 48th Street and maybe give Mom a few bucks for rent on occasion. He viewed us as less than he and the Hansell children. My mother had been married to Robert Hansell and had five boys and two girls. They were his grandchildren in his eyes, not us. Later on we will talk of the Hansell children. My mother, God bless her, was a great lady in my eyes. However, she could not pick a man to save her ass. I think my grandfather held it against my mother that my father was really an undesirable bastard.

The only thing memorable about Belmont Avenue was that my mother would allow the young woman who lived on the third floor to watch Jackie and me. I don't think we had sex with her, but I know she allowed us to see her whole body completely nude many times. We'd lived on Belmont Avenue for about a year when we moved. Donny was five, Jackie was nine, and I was seven. My father never did find us after Haverford Avenue, or maybe he didn't want to. I don't know for sure.

I would not see my father again until his death in 1974, in his coffin. The only reason I attended his services was to see if he had really died—and if he had hair. He did. At the time of this writing, I don't.

Bartram Village

FROM BELMONT AVENUE, WE MOVED to 5403 Eastwick Terrace, Apartment 1A, Bartram Village, in Southwest Philadelphia. The first thing I observed was that whites outnumbered blacks. We were not the minority. In writing this, it finally dawned on me that Jackie stopped fighting so much. Before we moved to the village, Jackie was constantly fighting because we were the only white kids in the neighborhood. Jackie was always protecting and defending Donny and me. He would fight anyone: girls, bigger kids, or gangs. Kids are cruel.

Bartram Village was managed by the Philadelphia Housing Authority. At that time, civil servants were a little more accountable for their actions. For the most part, they did a good job with this property. It was probably built in the early 1940s, and in 2005 it still looked pretty damn good (pictured next page). There were three-story buildings with concrete floors, walls, and ceilings, and with metal doors. They had metal kitchen cabinets. They were downright indestructible and that's why they lasted. All the residents had their own locker in the basement, where they could store their personal belongings without fearing that someone would steal from them. There was also an area where tenants could put their washers, and hang their clothes on lines, in the back of the buildings. There was a schedule of what days you could hang your clothes. One of the best things about the village was that the heat was good and the hot water was plentiful, unlike the other places we had lived.

I'm almost sure my sister Sophia was instrumental in getting my mother on the list for an apartment in Bartram Village. I believe our rent when we first moved to Bartram Village was $43 a month. We were receiving welfare, and I believe our check amount was somewhere in the area of $90 a month. Unfortunately, the check came once a month on the first, which meant that by the end of the month, my mother was really broke and we had no money for food. Thank God for the church on Christmas and Thanksgiving, because they are at the end of the month, when Mom was broke. I can recall one year when the church didn't come through, and my mother mixed corn, peas, and beans for our Thanksgiving meal. That was probably the worst we ever had because my sister didn't come through either.

It was about this time that Jackie and I learned that we had something that could make our life better, and that was the ability to work. We now knew, through work we could have a better life. Since Jackie was older, he would always get the jobs first. Jackie's first job was helping the milkman. He carried the milk in the carriers to the apartments. We would wake up very early in the morning, three or four o'clock, and walk to the train overpass on Elmwood Avenue to wait for the milkman. We would work for two or three hours, and he would give us 25 cents, which was a lot of money. From there we started delivering papers on Saturday night, The Philadelphia Inquirer. We had our specific routes, and people basically paid as we went. The district manager for the Inquirer would come to our house to collect the money from us. We did pretty well with that: the Sunday paper was 25 cents. From there we went to shining shoes. We had our own special route of Elmwood Avenue to about 64th Street and down Woodland Avenue to 52nd Street. We made pretty decent money, more than from the papers or the milkman. We tried to do the best we could because this was a repeat business. Most of our customers, I think, just downright liked us.

It was in the first or second year that we lived in Bartram Village that the welfare department took my brothers and sisters (the Hansells) to court to help support us. This created ill feelings that lasted for many years. They were required to pay two or three dollars a week or month; I'm not sure which. This was at a time when they were just starting their families, and they really didn't have any money to spare. This was about the time that Walter, probably just nineteen years old himself and in the United States Marine  Corps, started sending allotment checks to my mom. No more did the Hansell children have to worry about contributing for our welfare. Walter took on the full responsibility of caring for our upbringing.

I think now is the time to explain my brother Walter Hansell. He would go on to become the greatest male influence in my life. I will be eternally grateful for the sacrifices he made to make sure Jackie, Donny, and I (pictured above) would have a better chance to grow up to be stand-up citizens. For the next ten years, he virtually gave up his personal life to raise his three half-brothers. To refer to Walter as a "half-brother" is truly a poor choice of words, after what he did for Jackie, Donny, and me. I know there is no way I can repay him for the loss of his youth.

Living in the projects in the early 50s was a different experience for Jackie, Donny, and me. Bartram Village was right next to Bartram's Garden, which is where John Bartram did something great. I'm not absolutely sure as to what it was, but there were some very old houses and many different plants and bushes. People came from great distances to see this place. There was no concrete, no asphalt, just dirt and gravel, which made it nice. There were two bridges that connected different areas of the park. These bridges crossed the railroad tracks.

There's a story behind that as well. When hobos and bums used to walk the railroad tracks, we would drop bombs (rocks) from the bridges onto the hobos and bums, and then run like hell. Sometimes if you were in the park after sundown, you could see girls and guys "rolling in the hay."

I think you know what I'm talking about. We would throw rocks and sticks at them and then run. These were not young kids, and you could get hurt.

Bartram's Garden was bordered by the railroad tracks, Bartram Village, and the Schuylkill River. There really wasn't any traffic, and basically, you couldn't get hurt other than for annoying other people. The railroad tracks led to many different places. You could take the railroad tracks to Jerry's Corner (this was an old-fashioned farmers market) and play at the arcade if you had money. The railroad tracks would also take you to swimming holes (more like puddles of dirty water), where you could also fish for carp. Jackie was present when a kid who lived across the terrace drowned in one of these swimming holes.

The railroad tracks would also lead you to the city dump, where you could hunt rats. These rats would come out of fires, and we would beat them to death with sticks. I can remember one time when we were hunting rats at the dump, someone saw something shiny. There was a lot of pushing and shoving, and someone pushed me into a pile of metal banding tape that severely cut my forehead. My brother Jackie picked me up and carried me to the nearest highway, where he tried to flag someone down but no one stopped. I wouldn't have stopped either, because both Jackie and I were covered in blood, and we just would have messed up their car. Jackie carried me all the way home, where my mom gave medical attention to my injury and then beat the hell out of me for getting hurt. You could also hunt rabbits by setting traps along the tracks. We were never really very good at that.

We met many different people when we lived in the Village, and those five years would leave an indelible mark on our lives. There were six apartments in each building. We lived on the first floor, across the hall from Dotty. This young girl was really ugly. She always wanted to play doctor and nurse. On the second floor lived Petey Moore, who was a pretty smart kid, except he hung with Eddie Anderson, who was absolutely crazy and lived on the third floor.

I remember when Eddie thought he could make a parachute from a sheet. He jumped from the third-floor window with a sheet into a snowdrift on top of bushes and didn't get hurt. Another time, Eddie caught a rat at the dump. He brought the rat home and kept it in his locker in the basement. Eddie would feed the rat, and he claimed that the rat and he were friends. He put his hand in the box where the rat was. The rat bit down on his index finger and would not let go. You have to see these two little kids stomping on a rat's head with Eddie's finger in its mouth. We killed the rat and Eddie skinned it. I don't know whatever became of Eddie, but I do know he was sick in the head.

Also on the third floor lived Bobby Downey, his sister Betty Ann, and his brother Billy. The Downey family was the only family in the building that had a mother and father living together. That was somewhat unique in Bartram Village. Most tenants were women with children. You would have to say that the Downeys were as normal as normal could be in the projects. Something I recall about the Downey family is that Bobby would let us look at his sister with no clothes on. I think there was a hole in the bathroom door. When we were caught, Bobby and Betty Ann would fight like cats and dogs. Betty Ann was older than Bobby and she'd win.

The greatest thing about the Downey family was that they had a television set. Jackie and I loved to watch television. We would walk up to the third floor, and Jackie and I would argue as to who was going to knock on the door, and who was going ask if we could watch television. We had it timed to where we would ask after they had finished dinner.

We had other friends in the village; namely, Bobby Warner and his brother Richie. Everyone thought Richie was gay, but no one ever talked about it. Like just about everyone else, there was no father around the Warner home. Bobby Warner's nickname was "Moocher" because every time someone would have something to eat, Bobby would mooch. The name was given to him by Jimmy Deiter.

The Deiter family lived on Woodland Terrace. Their family was a shining example of the purpose of subsidized housing in the 1950s. Mr. Deiter was discharged from the military in the 1940s. He by then had six children, three boys and three girls. The girls were Eleanorann, Ruthanne, and Annamae. The boys were Buzzy, Joey, and Jimmy. Their family lived in Bartram Village and saved their money to buy a house. The house they bought was in Cherry Hill, New Jersey, off Kings Highway in Kingston Estates. Jimmy was more Jackie's friend. They would hang out and get in trouble, not serious trouble. I guess mischief would be a better word.

By now, there was a division between Jackie and me. For it was Jackie's opinion that if we got in trouble, the government would take Jackie, Donny, and me away from our mom. Jackie would say that two Pitts in a mess wouldn't look good. Therefore, I was not allowed to hang around with Jackie very often. This was before Walter was discharged from the United States Marine Corps.

Jimmy was the youngest boy in the Deiter family, and he would have Jackie, his best friend, come to their new house, after they'd moved to New Jersey, during the summers and spend a few weeks. One of the most outstanding things about Jimmy was that he was a real hard worker and a real earner. As a young boy in Cherry Hill, he delivered newspapers and then started cutting grass. Jimmy always had money. There used to be a fruit/custard stand on Kings Highway known as the Deuces. Jackie and Jimmy would break in through this little window and help themselves to custards. They would load up the paper basket on the bikes with fruit. Only once did they get caught, and Jimmy's reply was, "It's just a little fruit." Jimmy got his driver's license when he was seventeen. Jimmy would visit Jackie and me, when we lived in Levittown, in his father's '57 Chevy. He would let Jackie and me drive the Chevy around. When I was old enough to get my driver's license, he once made me race him. He was driving his friend's '57 Plymouth, and I was in his father's '57 Chevy. I damn near destroyed the vehicle when I lost control. I would never race Jimmy again. Jimmy and I would remain friends until his death at the age of sixty-six. The world is less of a place without Jimmy.

When we lived in the Village, we would take bike, bus, or trolley trips. Some of the most memorable were to my sister's, since she had moved from Lancaster Avenue to Lansdowne, Pennsylvania, a pretty decent middle-class neighborhood. Jackie and I and our friends would ride our bicycles and hang out on her lawn. Please picture this: five young, hoodlum-looking eleven-year-olds with the right leg of their pants rolled up because of no chain guard, just hanging out and talking loud. It embarrassed the hell out of my sister. On one of these trips, Jackie, our friends, and I found this little swimming hole around Lansdowne and Baltimore Avenues. I can recall a time when we decided to play hooky from school and go swimming. Well, the police caught me and called my mom. She had to take buses and trolleys to get to the police station to pick me up. She came in and hit me with her belt right across my face. The police had to stop her from beating me, and honestly speaking, I deserved it—but I did enjoy the swimming.

When Walter was discharged from the Marine Corps, he only lived in the projects for a short time. I've come to realize that Walter felt that it was below us (only because of his Marine Corps training), and he would not live there. Consequently, Walter made a deal with the landlord in Kensington, and we moved.

Kensington

From the projects in Southwest Philadelphia, Walter moved us to 2016 E. Huntingdon Street in the Kensington section of Philadelphia. Walter made some kind of deal where we would have reduced rent, but we would have to fix up the house. What an undertaking!

The first thing he had us do was to dig the basement deeper, and we put all this dirt in the backyard. We never finished the job. We had a coal furnace and a bucket-a-day hot water heater. The furnace went down the first winter, and we started using the bucket-a-day to heat the house. This meant no hot water to take a bath, and no shower unless it was a cold one. You had to heat the water and carry it up to the bathroom from the kitchen. The only good part of living on Huntingdon Street was that our neighbor had two daughters. Jackie and I would spend a lot of time peeping through the glass, looking at the two daughters who never pulled down the shades. Jackie and I got a good view all the time.

Kensington was a very rough neighborhood. It was white blue-collar. Several blocks away there were Hispanic and black neighborhoods. Whites, blacks, and Hispanics all went to the same school. I went to John Paul Jones Junior High. Jackie went to Daniel Boone. This was a special school for guys who couldn't or wouldn't behave in regular school. At John Paul Jones, I met some different people. These kids were really different than those in the projects, and honestly, we didn't make very many friends. We didn't live there that long. I remember Jackie having to take the EL train that ran above ground. On his way home from Daniel Boone, some of the guys in the neighborhood challenged my brother. Jackie had to take on one after another. Jackie got hurt pretty bad, but so did a lot of those guys. Jackie did well. Walter had Jackie go live with Walter's foster parents—Aunt Hattie and Uncle Joe—in Quakertown, Pennsylvania, to get him out of special school, which was a real break for Jackie.

Walter was then part of the truckers' union. He never really had a steady job. He would always work out of the truckers' union hiring hall, and there were a lot of times when there were no jobs for Walter.

When we lived on Huntingdon Street, the Durnin family came into our life. When Walter was discharged from the Marine Corps, he got a job at Fox Warehousing, a company in South Philadelphia, where he met Charlie Durnin. This was before Walter joined the truckers' union. Charlie and his family lived on Amber Street, only a few blocks away. Charlie introduced Walter to his family, and ultimately Jackie, Donny, Mom, and I got to know the Durnin family: big Charlie, Jean, Pat, Jeannie, Charlie, and Jackie (Reds). Charlie is still in my life, and I'm sixty-eight. At the time of this writing, I have to say Charlie is still one of my oldest friends. Reds fell by the wayside. He joined the carpenters' union and developed a real severe drinking problem that alienated him from his family for many years. I recently had the pleasure of having lunch with Charlie, his wife, Ruth, and Jackie. What great memories we shared. I lost track of Jeannie after her mother died. I believe she married someone from New Jersey, and I haven't seen her since. I understand she passed away a few years back.

Pat and my brother Walter ultimately were married, only after Jackie, Donny, and I were out on our own years later.

(Pictured left to right: "Big" Charlie, Walter, Pat, and Jean)

Big Charlie had recently gotten sober, for he was an alcoholic, and remained sober till his death many years later. I remember the first winter on Huntingdon Street, when we were really broke. I still see the picture of Pat and her mother Jean carrying pots of soup for our family. This is also the winter that we had to cut the cellar steps to feed the bucket-a-day furnace to heat the house, as we were out of coal. Thank God we made it through that period. The following year, my brother Bill and his wife Betty were getting divorced after they had just purchased a house in Levittown. Neither Bill nor Betty wanted the house; therefore, it was offered to Walter. Mom, by selling Jackie's, Donny's, and my insurance policies, could come up with the money to save the house from foreclosure.

CHAPTER 2

Levittown

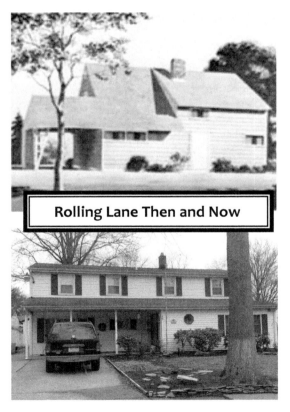

Rolling Lane Then and Now

I have thought for months on how to open "Levittown," since it had the greatest impact on my life. It opened a whole new world of thinking.

It was now 1960. Levittown was built starting sometime in 1953. The house we lived in was at 42 Rolling Lane, in the Red Cedar Hill section of Levittown. The house was probably built in 1955, and from our standpoint was considered new. It was a two-bedroom ranch with an unfinished attic. Mom had one bedroom. Jackie, Donny, and I had the other bedroom. Walter would sleep on the couch. The floors were all black 9" x 9" vinyl-asbestos tiles, which were broken around the perimeter of the house due to foundation settling problems. I came to realize this problem existed in all Levitt-built homes. The kitchen cabinets were metal, and not too many of them. The heater was in the bathroom, with a metal cover over it, and when it ran, it made a lot of noise. The bathroom was next to the main entrance. I could never figure that out. The exterior lot size was about 50 x 100 feet. My family and I viewed it as a mansion, after living in some of the places we had lived. The only drawback was that we still had furniture we were ashamed of—it was in very bad condition. We actually had boards under the cushions on the couch to keep them straight.

We still didn't have any money. We would not even have the house if it were not for my brother Bill and his ex-wife Betty abandoning it. They were prepared to let it go into foreclosure. My mother was always concerned about life insurance and having insurance policies on my brothers and me so we could have proper burials. She decided to sell our insurance policies to bring the mortgage current. The house would then belong to Walter. Walter was still working at the hiring hall. It seemed that things were picking up, and we would be able to keep up with the bills.

Levittown, when we moved there, was like a painter's blank canvas. The trees and shrubs were small; the streets were clean with ample parking and driveways, unlike the congestion of the city. I guess the biggest difference was the people: they came from all ethnic and economic groups.

Levittown was like a new beginning filled with hopes of things to come. One of the greatest differences we experienced was that people seemed to be naive. They actually left their valuables on their carports and not under lock and key. This was something different for us; in Kensington they'd steal whatever was not tied or locked down.

As I said earlier, we still didn't have any money. As a matter of fact, we could not afford to have our trash removed. Understand that in Levittown back then, you were responsible for paying for trash removal. This brings to mind Walter's good friend Nick Natoli, who also became my good friend. For some reason or other, Nick could not live at his parents' home on D Street in Philadelphia. I never asked why. Nick was driving Walter's car, a 1952 Buick, and throwing trash on the side of the road. (I now know at this stage of my life that was not a nice thing to do.) We got caught by the police and could not pay the fine. Instead, Nick spent three nights in jail.

Nick Natoli lived with us for about a year. In that year, he taught Jackie and me how to box. There was a kid in the neighborhood named Joe Bannon, who thought he was a real badass because he was in all kinds of sports in school, a real jock. He once challenged both Jackie and me to fight him at the same time. This would be a real embarrassment if we got beat, so it was decided that since I was a better boxer, I would fight Joe. I kicked his ass, only because of the training I had received from Nick. We learned a lot from Nick. Probably the most important thing we learned was to be honest. I remember often asking Nick what he would do in certain situations. You could speak to Nick about anything, and he would give you an honest answer.

Nick was getting over a girl that he loved, and for the life of me, I can't remember her name. He did get over her when he bought a horse. A big horse, seventeen hands high, and he boarded it at a local stable. It was about this time he met Diane. Diane was a friend of Pat's. By this time Walter and Pat had become a real item. Diane lived a few blocks from Pat on Amber Street in Philadelphia, with her mother, father, and brother Eddie. Diane wasn't really pretty, but she was reasonably attractive plus fun to be with, and she really loved Nick. They got married and rented an apartment in Philadelphia. Other than Diane, Nick had no luck at all. No sooner had they gotten married than Diane got pregnant and Nick got drafted into the United States Army and sent to Vietnam. I think it was then that Nick contracted some form of cancer. Agent Orange was being used at the time he was there. Two years after Nick was discharged, his young daughter was deformed by either scalding water or fire. She had to go through several operations to have a normal childhood. Nick and Diane then purchased a home in Williamstown, New Jersey, and lived there in peace and happiness working for the United States Postal Service.

Nick and I remained friends until his death in 1994. I still remember that very cold day in January when he was interred. I tried to keep in touch with Diane and spoke with her two or three times after Nick's death, but then she stopped answering or returning my calls. I still say good morning to Nick every day, along with the rest of my morning club.

One of the advantages of moving to Levittown was that my brother Jackie could move back home. Bristol Township (Pennsylvania) at that time had no special schools for bad kids. This meant Jackie would be going to regular school with Donny and me. Donny went to Thomas Jefferson Elementary School about a mile from our house. Jackie and I went to Benjamin Franklin Junior High School about three miles from our house. We all walked to Thomas Jefferson Elementary School, then Jackie and I would take the school bus to Benjamin Franklin Junior High School. This was the first time ever Jackie and I rode a free school bus.

In Philadelphia, Jackie would take the EL and I would walk to school. The EL was a train that traveled above the streets of Philadelphia. In the time that Jackie went to Daniel Boone special school, they didn't have grades, and since Jackie had repeated a few of them before he was sent to Daniel Boone, the Bristol Township School District put us in the same grade. The Philadelphia school system also had A and B semesters. You could start school in September or February, depending on your birthday. Jackie started school in September, a year and a half before I did. However, I started school in February, and that meant Jackie was three semesters ahead of me. Unfortunately, Bristol Township schools did not have A and B semesters, so instead of advancing me to the ninth grade, I was put in the eighth grade with Jackie.

Again, like everything else in Levittown, the schools were new. They didn't smell or have bugs. They were clean, bright, and cheerful, with new desks and adequate ventilation even in the men's room (boys' room). They had good heat and good teachers, for the most part. They were young and good at their jobs, and frankly, some of the female teachers looked good. Just like our neighbors, they, too, appeared to be naive. This was when I learned one of my most important things in life, when I heard Mr. Ruane, my science teacher, say that we did not have to follow the lesson plan. In his opinion, the lesson plan was merely a guide. From that day forward, I have always believed there is more than one way of doing anything. This became my way to approach any situation in life. Mr. Ruane; Mr. Tomaselli, the art teacher; and Mr. Russo, the history teacher, as Jackie and I would find out, were the disciplinarians in the school. Jackie was always getting whacked by one person or another.

The person I liked most in school was the school nurse, Mrs. Hayden. She was always nice to me. When I told her I was sick, she would send me home, sometimes without calling my mother or Walter to come to pick me up. I think she knew my mother would have to walk the three miles there and back, because my mother never got a driver's license. A close second to Mrs. Hayden was Mr. Diddo. I believe he was either the vice principal or the guidance counselor, or both. He always treated me respectfully, unlike other school officials. When I was ready to attend night school in Bayonne, New Jersey, in 1967, he was very helpful in obtaining my school records. He wished me luck. As he put it, and I quote, "I wish you luck in all your current and future endeavors," and he really meant it. This was one of the nicest things anyone had said to me to this point in my life. The only person I didn't like at Benjamin Franklin Junior High School was Mr. Nussman, the English teacher in ninth grade. He threw Bobby Warner and me out of the class for the entire year. Needless to say, I flunked English and spent the whole year in the auditorium with all the other students who'd been thrown out of class.

One of the most memorable things about attending Benjamin Franklin Junior High was that girls seemed to be very naive. I spent a lot of time scrounging desserts from the girls. This was before Walter arranged for us to have free lunches. Jackie and I would run to the lunchroom to be first in line so no one would know we were getting free lunches. Jackie and I really liked school lunches because our mother was a very poor cook. I'm not talking bad about her, it's the truth.

Getting back to scrounging food, there was a kid in school name Lewis Claytor, who was on the wrestling team. He also thought he was a badass, commonly known as a bully. For one reason or another, he thought I was scrounging his food from the girls and challenged me to a fistfight. This guy scared the living hell out of me. I worried about this upcoming fight all day. I was even sweating behind my kneecaps. When three o'clock came, there was such a large crowd outside, and I thought I was going to get killed. Lewis came at me in a wrestling stance, his arms raised slightly and his head looking down. This is when I kicked him in the face, and he went down. I continued to kick him until he gave up. Unfortunately for Lewis, he was raised in Levittown most of his life and, frankly, had no idea about street fighting the way I did being from Philadelphia. Lewis never gave me a hard time again.

I joined the track team in eighth grade to build up my legs. They were like sticks. Once at practice, I was hit with a shot-put. It nearly broke my hip. I ran the 100-yard dash, the 880 relay, and cross-country. I was pretty good.

There was a tall black guy, named Michael Steele, who went on to become a state champion. I recall we were at a meet with another school when he fell down, got up, and still beat me. That's when I quit the track team. I had always been a runner. So when we ran cross-country during gym, I would get ahead of everyone. Consequently, I would stand in the woods and smoke cigarettes. I used to smoke wherever I could. I smoked in the boys' room. I even smoked in the hallways, fanning my hand so no one could see where the smoke was coming from. I never got caught smoking.

One of the great things I did while attending Benjamin Franklin Junior High School was to set a record in pull-ups. As I recall, I did sixty-three of them. This was probably because I was so thin, weighing 115 pounds, and had very good upper-body strength.

Benjamin Franklin Junior High is where I met Karen Bailey. I was in the eighth grade, and she had some of the same classes. You could say Karen was one of my first true loves. She was my first true love until I met my second true love, Joyce, at Mr. Tomaselli's dance class. Yes, dance class—nothing in Philadelphia like dance class. Joyce was sexy and attractive. I remember she lived in the Dogwood section of Levittown. I would later find out that the Ku Klux Klan demonstrated in the Dogwood section in 1957. I would ride my bicycle from the Red Cedar Hill section to a spot near a canal close to her home. I felt like a little kid riding my bicycle to her house. She was the first girl I ever bought a Christmas gift for. I gave her an Elvis Presley Christmas album, and then I gave her a ring because we were going steady. Since she lived in Dogwood, she would attend Woodrow Wilson High School in ninth grade, while I still would be attending Benjamin Franklin Junior High School in ninth grade—something to do with maximum attendance in the schools. I guess it really wasn't love, because we broke up soon after the change in schools.

In the tenth grade, I also went to Woodrow Wilson High School. The only thing notable about that was I came in late to gym class. The gym teacher was so angry, he made me wrestle a kid by the name of Troxel, who outweighed me by almost a hundred pounds. He literally picked me up and threw me on the ground, and then he jumped on my head. I received a concussion and had to be taken to Delaware Valley Hospital, where I spent a few days. This is where I met a candy striper by the name of Sidra Newberg. She would affect my life unfavorably until this very day. You will hear a lot more about Sidra.

I think the first friend Jackie and I met was Joe Varano. His family lived on Robin Hill Lane, also in the Red Cedar Hill section of Levittown. He was a second-generation Italian-American who had moved from Tamaqua, Pennsylvania, the coal-cracking region. There were also two younger brothers, Tony and Tommy; Mr. and Mrs. Varano; and Nona. Nona is Italian for "grandmother." Joe would draw pictures of boats, with Nona leaning over the back being sick on her way from Italy. Joe always wanted to work on boats and to be at the seashore. I remember a time, when we could not have been more than thirteen or fourteen, we hitchhiked to Wildwood. We had no idea how to get there or how long it would take. It seemed to take forever. We stayed at Aunt Mary's for one day and came back. It was a trip I will never forget.

Joe's father was a barber who really didn't make much money. I think he had a problem with alcohol. According to Joe, his father's problem started in World War II. He was at the Battle of Kasserine Pass in Tunisia in North Africa. This was the first battle of the American armored division in World War II, and we were defeated soundly by Field Marshal Rommel, the great German field marshal. Mrs. Varano was a stay-at-home mom. I never got to know Tony very well, and Tommy even less because he was that much younger. Joe was a real popular guy. I don't think there was anyone in school that disliked Joe. He was a real good-looking kid with black curly hair. He was always ready to hang out and get into some kind of mischief.

Joe, Jackie, and I were probably the first members of the Red Cedar Hill "Gang." To call it the Red Cedar Hill Gang was an exaggeration of the word "gang." We were now considered suburbanites and not city kids anymore. The most we ever did was maybe shake a light pole until the light went out, or stand on a street corner. Sometimes we would go to the pharmacy and steal goodies and cigarettes, or maybe throw snowballs at cars or be insulting to people, but we would run if they ever came after us. We were very lucky to never get caught.

When we attended school, drugs were not readily available. However, two grades below us, drugs began to run rampant. Unfortunately, Tony started dabbling in drugs, and one cold winter night he overdosed. His creepy friends decided not to take him to the hospital but to leave him on his front lawn without telling anyone, and Tony died. To this day, I still say good morning to him. At the time of this writing I'm sixty-six years old, and Joe and I are still very good friends.

I next met Johnny Tollan, shortly after meeting Joe. Johnny was younger than I and a good guy. He also became a member of the Red Cedar Hill Gang, even though he lived in the Crabtree section of Levittown. He lived with his mom, dad, older sister, and brother. They lived in a Levittowner-type house, which was an upgrade by one model. It was one level with three bedrooms. They had this old Packard that no one drove. John's father was ill, so I never saw him leave the house. They also had no money. Johnny and I are still good friends. A few years ago Johnny moved to South Florida.

It is now 1963 and in Pennsylvania you could get your driver's license when you were sixteen years old. Naturally, on my sixteenth birthday I got my license, and I do mean on my birthday. Johnny got his license shortly after; his first car was a '54 Mercury. My brother Walter allowed me to drive the '52 Chevy we owned. Johnny and I would race. Johnny would always win. The '52 Chevy we owned was kind of a hand-me-down from all my brothers. I think my brother Bill purchased it. I don't know when he gave it to my brother Walter, who in turn gave it to my brother Jackie, who then gave it to me. Walter had ruined it long before Jackie and I had it. Walter was really hard on vehicles, always wanting to race with nothing under the hood.

Jackie and I would take the '52 Chevy to school and always had to park on a hill, because the only way it would start would be to push and pop the clutch. We got real good at starting it. It burned almost as much oil as gas. The only way you knew how much gas was in the vehicle was by subtracting the mileage and then adding the gas purchase, because the gas gauge didn't work either. So every day, we had to check the oil. Jackie started using the '52 Chevy to make paper deliveries on Sunday until he bought his '55 Dodge, and then I became the proud driver of the '52 Chevy. I know for a fact when I first got the vehicle. I would be pushing away the snow just to wash and wax the car. That's how crazy I was.

When we first moved to 42 Rolling Lane, there were two osteopaths who had offices in a regular rancher across the street from our house. Jackie and I got the job of washing their one standard-shift, push-button-drive Rambler because their driveway was steep. I remember Jackie or me—it was probably me—not being able to get the vehicle back up their steep driveway. Jackie could drive a standard transmission. It was really embarrassing. As I'm writing this in the year 2013, the osteopaths are still across the street from 42 Rolling Lane, but with a greatly expanded rancher and a large parking lot.

I got to be pretty good at driving a standard transmission. As a matter of fact, by the age of fourteen or fifteen I was stealing Walter's '52 Ford. Not knowingly, Walter taught me how to be a sneak. For you see, Walter would take chalk and mark the tires on the driveway, while I just bought my own chalk and made my own marks.

I don't mean to jump ahead, as I am trying to keep this in some kind of order. I feel now is the time to write about my running away. I was forbidden to drive the '52 Chevy across any bridge because you were not allowed to push vehicles across bridges, and there was always a fear of the vehicle breaking down. I had been sixteen for about a month, which meant I'd had my driver's license for just as long, when Walter pissed me off so bad I decided to run away. My runaway destination was not close. I figured I would go to Florida, because I hated the cold weather, and then go to Texas. I did accomplish the first leg. I drove down Route 1, because Interstate 95 did not exist. I then picked up hitchhikers along the way to get money to buy fuel and oil.

In Jacksonville, Florida, I came to a bridge, but did not have any money for the toll. At that point, I had not eaten in two days and I was hungry. I went to a church begging for help. The minister gave me a food coupon for a local restaurant, where I ate. I then went to a junkyard to sell the '52 Chevy and buy a motorcycle to go to Texas. The owner of the junkyard would not buy the '52 Chevy because I didn't have the title, but he did allow me to sleep in the junkyard. The next day, he told me about a new restaurant opening in Jacksonville, McDonald's, where I might be able to find a job. I always looked older than my age, so I just told people I was eighteen, and no one asked for identification. I got the job and, man, did I eat. I would work at McDonald's during the day and in the early evenings, and then drive back to the junkyard to sleep.

I met another guy at McDonald's, and I shared with him that I was sleeping at the junkyard. He took me back to his house and introduced me to his mom, and she allowed me to stay with them for a few bucks. Their apartment was in public housing, commonly referred to as "the projects," the same thing that we moved out of in Southwest Philly, but it sure as hell beat the junkyard. I stayed there for a couple weeks.

I decided that I really didn't want to work at McDonald's the rest of my life, so I called Walter and told him that I wanted to come home. He in turn called the Jacksonville Police Department, and they came and picked me up. I think I should note that in 1963 in Jacksonville, the police station was segregated. There were separate cells, drinking fountains, and bathrooms for "white" and "colored." I really didn't want to stay at the police station, so at the age of sixteen I convinced the Jacksonville police to let me go. They did. Walter flew down, and we drove back in the '52 Chevy. We drove straight through, which meant I had to drive at the times he slept. I remember being very tired and closing my eyes for short breaks, which continually extended longer. I got up to about twenty seconds of closing my eyes, when I fell asleep. The next thing I knew, the Chevy was bouncing around in a field. Thank God, neither Walter nor I, or the Chevy, was hurt or damaged.

Getting back to the friends in Levittown, I would be remiss in not talking about Bill Ridgeway, commonly known as Ridgee. He and I were in the same grade and were the same age. His family lived on Red Cedar Drive. I think there were six children plus his mom and dad. His mom was a stay-at-home mom and his father worked. I don't think he had a good job, or a good-paying job, and I think he also had a drinking problem. It seems to me, looking back, they had no more than we did.

Ridgee was always being thrown out of his house by his father, even though he was only fourteen years old. His pop was a real piece of shit. The reason I distinctly remember that is, the first time Ridgee walked to our house, it was a cold and rainy winter night and he had no coat. This scene would be repeated time and time again. Sometimes he would spend nights at our house. Ridgee could not dress, maybe because they didn't have any money for clothing, but I really think, even with money, he still couldn't dress.

He was a real loyal friend. He was also a member of the Red Cedar Hill Gang. That term still makes me laugh. We were friends the entire time I lived in Levittown, and somehow, after I left Levittown, we lost communication and to this day I regret that. I understand Ridgee served three tours of duty in Vietnam, and had attained a good rank when he was discharged from the United States Army. He got married, had several children, and lived in the Bucks County (Pennsylvania) area until he passed away in 2004. Unfortunately, I did not find out about his passing until he was in the ground, and I never had the opportunity to pay my last respects to an old and dear friend. I say good morning to him every morning.

Another good friend was Jimmy Cook. Jimmy lived in a Levittowner in the Goldenridge section of Levittown with his mom, dad, and younger brother. I think Jimmy's dad had a good job. I believe his mom worked as well, because I started to drink at his house when no one was home. Drinking at the age of fourteen is considered a rite of passage for young men. I remember a New Year's Eve party at Jimmy's house. Two girls, Jimmy, and I, drinking sloe gin fizzes. My God, did I get sick! I remember standing on our carport practicing how to walk a straight line to get by my mother. My mom was always inside our house waiting for me. Somehow, she always caught me and beat the hell out of me. She had warned us time after time about drinking.

I couldn't have been more than fifteen when Jimmy introduced me to his cousin Karen Smith, who was seventeen. Karen was beautiful and built well, plus she smelled great. She had a driver's license and a car. We went out a few times, and I thought I'd died and gone to heaven. I was to learn later that it was a ploy, for she had just broken up with her nineteen-year-old boyfriend, and she was trying to make him jealous. I never realized how close I came to getting my head beat in. I remember bringing Karen to our house, and my brother Walter making a play for her. When I left Levittown, I would never see Karen again, nor her cousin Jimmy Cook. Jimmy, as I understand it, went to the West Coast and became a hippie. We are talking the '60s, and that's when the hippie movement started.

I never stopped hanging out on Red Cedar Drive with the guys. One summer night when I was sixteen, we met two new girls in the neighborhood, Franny and Sandy. They were sisters who had just moved from Philadelphia. Their friend Dolly Spor also came to hang out on the drive. This is when Dolly came into my life. She was the complete package: looks, brains, humor, and body. This is when I fell in love with her, and she with me. I took her home to meet my mom, and she took me to Philadelphia to meet her mom and family. They lived on Vista Street in Northeast Philadelphia. Dolly had three brothers, one sister, and one adopted sister. Her mother and father were divorced, and her mother's boyfriend Johnny, who lived with them. Dolly's mother's name was Marge, and she insisted I call her Marge. I guess that is where Dolly got her sense of humor. Her mother was one real funny lady, and I had the honor of knowing Marge until her death in 2006. I say good morning to her also.

I don't know what happened to Johnny, or Dolly's adopted sister or older brother Sonny, except to say that Sonny went on to become an alcoholic and, to his credit, stayed sober for the last twenty-five years of his life. He passed in 2007. I was told this by Jimmy in early 2014. Her brother Al, who also had a great sense of humor and was fun to be with, was always sickly and died in his mid-fifties in 2002. I say good morning to him also. Her older sister Sissy, in my opinion, has had a rough life. She moved into an area known as Bristol Terrace. This is a horrible, crime-filled neighborhood as of this writing in 2013. She still lives in that neighborhood.

One of the benefits of knowing Dolly was that I got to meet her brother Jimmy Spor. Jimmy and I shared the same birthday, February 2, but he was a year older than I. Up until the time of his death, we spoke at least a few times a year and on our birthdays. When I got my driver's license, Walter would not let me use the '52 Chevy. Jimmy lent me his '52 Mercury to take his sister out. It was wintertime and there was ice on the ground. I almost smashed his vehicle, and he never even got angry about it. Jimmy was a good-looking guy who was dating Franny, one of the girls who had just moved from Philadelphia. Jimmy had quit school at sixteen and gotten a decent job making decent money. He dressed well, talked well, and took no shit from anyone, but God, he could exaggerate. His relationship with Franny worked out much better than my relationship with Dolly. For you see, she sent me a Dear John letter when I was in Marine Corps boot camp. Jimmy and Franny got married and had a few children, but then they got divorced. I think Jimmy went on to have three more wives.

In my opinion, Jimmy only got lucky with his last wife, Taisi. Other than Taisi, Jimmy could not pick and keep a woman to save his ass. At one of Jimmy's weddings, I had the opportunity to dance with his sister Dolly, and I realized how thankful I was that my relationship with Dolly didn't work. Both of us were completely different people than we were when we were younger, and in love sometimes you luck out. Jimmy and Taisi took care of Jimmy's mom, Marge, for the last few years of her life, for the most part. A couple years after her death, they moved to Florida. I miss seeing Jimmy. In September 2014 Jimmy passed away from throat cancer. When I last spoke to Jimmy, he told me he had five to nine months. He shared with me that the doctor had suggested chemotherapy. When Jimmy asked if it would add to his life, the doctor said probably not, so Jimmy declined to have chemotherapy. I figured I had little time to make arrangements to go down to Florida to see Jimmy within a few weeks. His wife Taisi called me and informed me that Jimmy did get the chemotherapy and, unfortunately, had died. I truly hope that if I were ever in the same situation, I would not allow doctors to do something that I didn't want done.

I opened this chapter with a statement that Levittown was a diverse community—ethnically, economically, and religiously. In 1954 a brand-new home sold from $5,500 to $12,000, and basically all the homes in a particular section were the same price. You would have to go to a different section to buy a better or lesser house. We lived in one of the lowest-priced sections in Levittown. However, we attended schools with kids from more-expensive sections. That's how it became diverse. The only real surprise was the lack of black people. I don't think there were any living in Levittown, except for Bristol Terrace, where there were no whites. In school, we would meet Jews, Catholics, Protestants, blacks, whites, Hispanics, and an assortment of Asians. Ironically, everyone got along. From my experience in Philadelphia, this was unusual.

I mentioned Sidra Newberg earlier and said that she's affected my life to this day. Sidra was a year and a half younger than I. She was not pretty, but she was attractive. She took full advantage of all of her attributes: she had great legs, beautiful breasts, a great butt, and long straight black hair. She could really put on makeup, she dressed impeccably, she wore good perfume, and she was funny. She just about threw herself at me after meeting in the hospital. For some reason, it appeared she wanted to be accepted by the bad kids. She considered me a bad kid when she gave herself to me of her own free will. I'm almost positive she was a virgin. The only thing I felt bad about was that I didn't really care enough for her to deserve what she gave me. As I got older, I realized how cruel young people are. We would play hooky from school at her girlfriend Susan's house. Sidra was in the Neshaminy School District and went to a different school. She introduced me to some of her friends, but for the most part, they were middle-class and a little snooty. Sidra lived in the Cobalt Ridge section of Levittown in a Jubilee-type home. This was one step below the most-expensive homes in Levittown. Her family wasn't hurting at all. She lived with her two younger brothers: Chet, who I thought had challenges, and Brian, who also shared Sidra's feeling of being less than others, in my opinion. I never could understand it. Sidra will be mentioned many times in this story.

Sidra's mother, Shirley, was an uptown lady. She kept a beautiful home. She was a great cook and a pretty woman. Somehow, I don't think she liked me initially, and for years she didn't like me. The greatest benefit from meeting Sidra was meeting her father, Jack. Jack would become one of the most important men in my life at that time. I know Jack liked me. He took Sidra and me to my first James Bond movie. He never asked me for a cent. He even bought the refreshments. He always treated me with the utmost respect—not that I deserved it. In turn, I paid Jack the most respect I've ever shown to anyone. When he found out that I was fatherless, he attempted to give me fatherly advice. Honestly speaking, I didn't know how to deal with someone who treated me as if I counted. This was a new feeling for me. I loved that man for it, and did accept his advice. I could not believe that he had no problem with me dating his daughter. Shirley and Jack had more class than I could ever hope to get at that stage of my life.

Jack and Shirley were from Brooklyn, New York, and when they took trips to Brooklyn, they invited me along. Looking back, I understand that they were really liberal. I know that both Jack and Shirley demonstrated in Washington, D.C., for civil rights. I remember one time that my brother Jackie and I were going to pour a concrete slab patio for Jack and Shirley. We dug this big hole for the foundation and never finished the job. Later in life, I would do a much bigger job for Jack and Shirley.

**Standing left to right: Bob, Walt, Bill, Ted, and Stanley
Seated left to right: Donny, Harvey, Bobbie, Sophia, and Jack**

I think it's time that I explained my family and my relationship with my mother, Ruth Roberta Harvey. By the time I was born, my mother was running out of male names, so she named me her maiden name, Harvey. To add insult to injury, she gave me the middle name "Morris" after the doctor who cared for me after my birth, Morris Neisser.

She married Robert Hansell. They had seven children, in age order: Sophia, William, Robert, Stanley, Walter, Roberta, and Theodore. When Mr. Hansell and my mother broke up, she married my father, Ruben Lee Pitts. They had three children, in age order: Jackie, me, and Donny.

There are more on my father's side, but that's part of another story. At no time did all the children live in one house. There were twenty-one years between Sophia and Donny. The most I remember at any one time was six, and that was in the Levittown house.

There are more on my father's side, but that's part of another story. At no time did all the children live in one house. There were twenty-one years between Sophia and Donny. The most I remember at any one time was six, and that was in the Levittown house.

When we first moved to Levittown—Walter, Jackie, Donny, Mom, and I—it soon became apparent that Walter and Mom were not going to get along. If Mom saw green, Walter saw yellow. Their relationship soon deteriorated. One or the other would have to leave, and after about a year and a half, Mom moved to my sister Sophia's in Morton, Pennsylvania. She really had no other option, because under no circumstances could she stay in Levittown, and she could not take Jackie, Donny, and me out of Bristol Township schools. Back then, it was a good school district. Furthermore, she had no way to support us.

After Mom moved, Bill was the first to move in. He was having real problems with his second wife, Terry. Ultimately, they did get divorced after Bill lived at 42 Rolling Lane. My brother Stanley also moved in because he was having problems with his wife, Marge. This created a whole new setup for us. Jackie, Donny, and I became slaves, and that's what they called us. Jackie was Bill's slave, which meant that Jackie would have to wash and iron Bill's clothes, make his bed, pack his lunch, and do different chores around the house. I was Stanley's slave and had to do the same thing. Walter had Donny as a slave. I guess I had the best deal, because Stanley wasn't hard on things. Bill wasn't hard on things either. Walter, on the other hand, was hard on everything. He was difficult to please.

The housekeeping chores led me and Jackie to our last fistfight. I'm not sure if I walked over the floor that he had just waxed or he walked on my floor, but he punched me in the face. I fell back and cut my back on the chain on the door. In turn, I punched him in the stomach. He bent over a little in a crouched position. I locked my hands and came down on the back of his head. I had no idea that a vase was there when his head came back up. It was a bloody mess. I thought he might lose his eye, for his head went into the vase and it cut around his eye. We told Walter that Jackie had slipped; if the truth were known, Walter would have beaten the hell out of both of us. That was Jackie and my last fight, thank God. I was a better boxer, but Jackie was always tougher. This living arrangement only lasted maybe nine months. The only good thing to come out of it was that Stanley and Bill contributed money to the household, which meant we ate better and the bills got paid. One thing I always said, while other kids were looking for fulfillment, my brothers and I were looking for dinner.

My ghostwriter, Bert, keeps asking me why Donny is not mentioned a lot up to this point in the book. It was somewhere between Bartram Village, Huntingdon Street, and early Levittown that we realized that Donny was somewhat different. When I say different, I mean that he was sissified to a degree, which I'm ashamed to say would lead me and Jackie not to let him hang around with us because of the neighborhood we grew up in. If you had a friend or family member who was different and who hung around with you, you must be different as well. No one wanted to be classified as that status.

I am ashamed to say that I ignored Donny until I was almost thirty-five years old, due to the street mentality that I acquired in Bartram Village and Huntingdon Street. At the age of thirty-five, I came to the conclusion that if someone else had a problem with Donny, it was their problem, not mine. This turned out to be one of the best decisions I've ever made, because Donny became my favorite brother. He was warm, loving, understanding, and considerate. I still had problems with his friends, but if I didn't welcome them to my home, Donny probably wouldn't have come. He would either bring my sister Sophia (above with Mom) or his friends, and always brought something from Termini Brothers Bakery in South Philadelphia. Donny was included much more in my life after I turned thirty-five years old.

We were always doing something around that house, not knowing that the talents we were learning—such as painting, drywall, electric, plumbing, and carpentry—would be useful. Walter had us doing everything. It reminds me of the time when Jackie and I were holding drywall on the ceiling, and Walter wasn't nailing too fast. Jackie and I were getting tired, so the board moved a little bit. Walter took his hammer and beat us across the feet. As I got older, I came back to work at 42 Rolling Lane prior to and after Walter's death.

Walter was, in fact, the disciplinarian, and if we stepped out of line, he had no problem with knocking the hell out of us. The punishment could be anywhere from you just couldn't go out to his kicking your ass. One of his favorite ways of punishing us was cutting our hair, and he was not a good barber. Long hair was just coming into style in the early 60s. Sometimes he just took our cigarettes. He did allow us to smoke when we were young. I think he did because he could bum cigarettes from us.

One very important thing that I should mention, Walter created a feeling that whenever he was around, no matter what kind of problems we had, things would be all right and we would get through it. In the entire time that Walter was our guardian, I never felt despair or helplessness. I always knew that Walter would take care of it, and I have striven all my life to create that feeling for other people. This was one of the greatest gifts from Walter.

Getting back to my return from Florida, Walter and I had this big argument, and I was told to leave. He'd had it with my shenanigans. I first moved to Camden, New Jersey, right off Federal Street, with a woman Mom made me call Aunt Agnes. This did not work out. She really didn't have any room. I then moved to Westmont, New Jersey, with Phil and Mary Palillo. They were friends of my mom, and I had known them for many years. I paid them $25 a week and slept in the attic. I lied about my age and got a job at West Jersey Hospital in Camden, as an orderly in the OR cleaning the operating rooms. The job really sucked, and to get there, I had to walk two miles to the bus stop on Haddon Avenue for the 25-minute bus ride. This was in March 1963. I was sixteen years old.

By April of 1963, I had saved enough money ($25) to buy a '52 Chevrolet, commonly referred to as a shitbanger, but it got me around, and it beat the bus. It also gave me the ability to get a part-time job, which I did—at Gino's Hamburgers on Route 70 in Haddonfield, New Jersey. Unfortunately, neither job paid very much money.

I was sixteen when I moved to New Jersey. State law required me to be seventeen to have a driver's license in New Jersey, so I went to the local DMV in Berlin, New Jersey, and applied for a driver's license in Jackie's name and got one. I had the Chevy a few months, but I really didn't like the car. I saw a '57 Ford for $300. I didn't have $300, so I went to my sister Sophia's house in Morton to see if she would lend me the money. I promised to pay her back within a few months, which I did. Ironically, when I borrowed the money from Sophia, her husband Walter was there, and he agreed to lend me the money.

Later, I would find out that Sophia and Walter were separated, and had been separated for quite some time. Sophia had kept this from the family for years. Ultimately, they were divorced and that broke my sister's heart. I don't think she ever got over Walt. I'm positive she never fell in love again. Sophia and Walter did have a son named Gary, and had a daughter Lisa right before the separation. I cannot imagine how hard it was for my sister to maintain her house and children and later my mom. When Mom first moved in with her, she was only there a short time. The second time was a lot longer and without the help of a man. But Sophia did it, and did it well. My sister is amazing.

I took the $300 and bought the 1957 Ford Fairlane 500 with the 292 V-8 engine. I loved that car. After leaving work at the hospital one day, I saw this beautiful girl walking down Haddon Avenue in Camden. The next thing I knew, I had pushed one car into two other cars and creat-  ed a large accident. I still remember thinking my car was bleeding as the water ran from the radiator to the ground.

This was the beginning of a fifteen-year ordeal. In 1963 auto insurance was not required in the state of New Jersey. That did not stop people from suing, and

I was sued for $3,200. New Jersey had what was called the Unsatisfied Claims Bureau, which paid Mrs. Chambers, the person who'd sued me for $3,200. I made arrangements with the Unsatisfied Claims Bureau to pay $8 a month, based on my income at that time, until the debt was paid. I had to pay the $8 a month or else I would lose my privilege to drive. I was smart enough to give them my real driver's license and not the one I got in Jackie's name.

After fifteen years of paying $8 a month, the State of New Jersey sent me a letter indicating that they wanted to change the agreement. I naturally responded with "No! A deal's a deal." The state then wrote back and said they would apply everything I had paid to the principal if I would pay it off. I replied and said, "I'd be interested in that." They in turn said I had paid somewhere around $850. I wrote and told them my records indicated I had paid them over $1,400, and if I had not paid them one month, they would've taken my driver's license, so I knew I'd never missed a payment. They wrote back and said they would agree with my number if I would pay it off, which I did, in the amount of $1,800. Since the accident happened close to the hospital, employees of the hospital were made aware that I was only sixteen. I, in turn, lost my job.

This was midsummer 1963, and I really wanted to move back to Walter's house in Levittown. I called him and he agreed to allow me to come back without a job or anything else. When I came back to Levittown, I dated Dolly and Sidra. It was a good time: my love for Dolly was getting stronger, and my need for Sidra was just as strong. I guess I should mention now that I'd quit school when I got thrown out of the house in March of 1963. I had no option; I had to get a job. If I'd just stayed in school two and a half months longer, I would've been in eleventh grade. This decision cost me later on. Walter made it clear that I had to get a job and give him $25 a week for room and board.

I searched everywhere for a job and got one in Croydon, Pennsylvania, at Owens-Illinois box factory, working the midnight shift. Here again I had to lie about my age, but I always looked older than I was. I think I made $1.25 per hour. The agreement with the State of New Jersey had not been made yet, and I didn't have the right to register a vehicle. I didn't get my right to register a motor vehicle until I was discharged from the United States Marine Corps and the deal with the state was consummated. Consequently, I made arrangements with one of the fellows at Owens-Illinois that I would meet him at his house, which was about a mile from 42 Rolling Lane. I would walk or hitchhike at 10 o'clock at night to make sure I was at this fellow's house at 11 Elizabeth Commons for my ride to work. I paid him two dollars a week. I remember he had a 1957 Oldsmobile standard-transmission V-8. This was one unique quick car. We got paid on Saturday morning at the factory, and people would go across the street to the local tavern, including the guy I rode with daily. They would cash my check at the bar. Although I was only sixteen years old, they would sell me drinks.

I had made the decision, after getting into such chaos with cars and courts, that I would join the Marine Corps on my seventeenth birthday. My brothers Walter and Ted had served in the Marine Corps. As a matter of fact, Ted was still in the Marine Corps. I didn't go back to school in September, knowing that in February I would be enlisting. According to my brother Walter, he'd rather have a sister in the whorehouse than a brother in the Army. I truly believed I would do better in the Marine Corps. You see, the competition was not as great as in the Army, Navy, or Air Force. The Coast Guard didn't count. In the mid-1960s, judges would give you the option of enlisting in the Marine Corps or going to jail. Most picked the Marine Corps, and it was one of the best decisions I've made.

You could enlist in the United States Marine Corps for three years, and that was what I did on my seventeenth birthday. Mom and I went to a location on Broad Street in Philadelphia, where she signed papers because I was under eighteen. However, I flunked the physical. I believe they said I had too much albumin in my urine. I went to the two osteopaths across the street from 42 Rolling Lane, and I was told not to eat eggs for a week and go back and take the physical. I didn't eat eggs for a week. I did go back and passed the physical and was sworn in by February 10, 1964.

The United States Marine Corps was something I never expected. We were taken by train from Philadelphia to Yemassee, South Carolina, and then bussed to Parris Island, South Carolina. When we got off the train, two drill instructors directed us onto a bus with a lot of cursing and yelling. I was scared to death, just as everyone else was. Before we got on the bus, they made us clean their barracks. If I thought that was bad, when we actually got to the Marine Corps recruit depot, it was sheer hell. Everyone seemed to be yelling at us, "Tighten up, tighten up." They said we were next to the lowest thing on earth. The lowest thing on earth was whale shit, and that was at the bottom of the ocean.

When I enlisted, I weighed 117 pounds. Within twelve weeks, I weighed 165 pounds. At chow, all the skinny guys were called to the front of the line and told to eat fast so they could get at the back of the line and get a second portion, which I did. Most of the time after chow, I would have to do PT (physical training). Generally, I would throw up. I don't know where all that weight and all that muscle came from, but it was there. I excelled in boot camp. I learned at that point that I had an IQ of 139. I was told that to be a genius, you had to have 140, and to go to OCS (Officer Candidates School), you needed 120. I have no idea why my MOS (military occupational specialty) was infantry.

My first job in boot camp was house mouse, which meant I was responsible to the drill instructor for running errands and things of that nature. From there I was made squad leader and ultimately the platoon right guide, because of my ability to run and my stamina. In 1964 drill instructors did hit you. I think I got hit every day with everything from a fist to a footlocker. I refused to show weakness. I got the Leatherneck Award out of boot camp. Only two men out of seventy-five would get this award. It was dress blues, and also commonly known as the Honor Man Award.

I excelled with a rifle. We practiced with an M1 and qualified with an M14. It was at the rifle range in our ninth week of training that I was recruited by three individuals in civilian clothing. I was sworn to secrecy, and to this day I'm obligated to that secrecy. After boot camp, I was assigned to L Company, 3rd Battalion, 8th

Marine Regiment, commonly known as L-3-8, where I was immediately assigned to a status known as TAD (temporarily assigned duty). By November 1964 I had taken the attitude that I would not do what the Marine Corps told me to do. The Marine Corps then gave me an honorable discharge with full benefits. Please note that I still keep the secret and will take it to my grave.

It was in advanced infantry training at Camp Geiger in Camp Lejeune, North Carolina, where I really got to know my brother Ted. The rule in Camp Geiger was that someone had to come and sign you out for liberty. My brother Ted was a Sergeant E-5 stationed at Cherry Point, North Carolina, and he came down and signed me out for liberty. We went to Jacksonville, North Carolina, and I got drunk as a skunk. Keep in mind, I was still only seventeen. Before I got drunk, I had the opportunity to speak to Ted and get to know him. He then moved up from last place to above many of my other brothers as a favorite. You will hear more about Ted in this story.

As soon as I'd enlisted in the Marine Corps, I immediately signed up for my mother to receive allotment checks. I think the rule was that I would kick in $43 and the government would kick in $43, which gave my mother a check for $86 a month. She really needed it. This meant that I would receive $25 per pay. In the Marine Corps you were paid twice a month, and in 1964 with no pay other than a PFC's, pay was $93 a month. For the month that I was in Camp Lejeune in L38, I was always broke. Later on, I would receive additional pay based on my new temporary duties, commonly known as hazardous duty pay. It still wasn't much.

One of the important things I learned in the Marine Corps was that just about any goal was attainable. "Improvise, adapt, and overcome" was right up there with "We do not have to follow the lesson plan" from junior high school.

Semper Fi

CHAPTER 3

My First Marriage

AFTER BEING DISCHARGED FROM THE Marine Corps, I had to find a place to live. Living with Walter was no longer an option, as Walter and Pat had gotten married since I had joined the Marine Corps. Jackie had married his first wife, Tina, and moved out. Donny, who'd always had problems with Walter, had some kind of argument and moved in with Jackie. Later, Donny would move from Jackie's, and he disappeared from our lives for a few years. God only knows where he went for those years. Shame on me, I didn't try to find him. I had to find a place to live and a job.

The job was easy to find. I went back to Owens-Illinois and worked the midnight shift again. When I returned to Owens-Illinois, I had to show them my discharge papers. They found out I was just eighteen then, but they still took me back. I had the same night superintendent, John Nicoletti, who, when I first worked at Owens-Illinois, made me the butt of all his jokes, probably because I was young and didn't know how to defend myself. I learned then that if you allowed people to take advantage of you, they would never stop. When I came back, he attempted to do the same thing again. I, in turn, was not ready to take his nonsense anymore and made that very clear to him. I was no longer going to be taken advantage of, and he stopped his games.

I found an apartment at 921 Wood Street in Bristol, Pennsylvania, a rear apartment. Since I had been supporting my mother, she moved in with me, and everything seemed to be going very well. I resolved my issue with the State of New Jersey, my 1963 accident, and got my right to register a vehicle back. I could then buy and drive a vehicle, this time with auto insurance. I was making every attempt to regain a relationship with Dolly, but wasn't getting very far. In the meantime,

I was also dating Sidra, for other reasons. I had been out of the Marine Corps for about two months when I finally got through to Dolly, and had the opportunity to start dating her again.

I called Sidra to tell her good-bye. When she said I couldn't tell her good-bye, I asked why and she told me she was pregnant and the doctor had confirmed it. My world came to an end. I spoke to my mom, and this was going to be the only time she gave me bad advice. She said, and I quote, "Son, you've made your bed, now you must sleep in it." She was saying I had to marry Sidra. At that time I was eighteen years old. Sidra was sixteen. We got married May 8, 1965. Sidra would be seventeen on the Fourth of July 1965.

To call it a "wedding" would be a misuse of the word. It may have been a joyous occasion for Sidra, but not for me. As a matter of fact, I worked the midnight shift the morning of the wedding. We were married in front of a justice of the peace with Sidra's immediate family present. To this day, I still don't understand why Jack and Shirley didn't know that she was pregnant, or claimed to be pregnant, because, in my opinion, they had enough class not to allow a sixteen-year-old daughter to marry white trash like me. Thank God, the wedding was not in front of a rabbi or minister, for Sidra was "Jewish in culture," as she would say, and I was Lutheran. Because it wasn't religious, it would be helpful later.

Later on we drove to New York for a honeymoon in Brooklyn. We weren't old enough to drink, or even to go to any fancy restaurant or anything really nice, so we spent time visiting her family. On our honeymoon she had what I thought was her period, which she claimed was a miscarriage. I never believed it, but being young and dumb, I decided to try to make things work. This meant that we would be living in the apartment on Wood Street with Mom. This wasn't going to work because Mom and Sidra were always fighting about anything and everything. Mom was upset because she knew of the pregnancy, and couldn't understand why Sidra took the liberties that she took. I truly believe that Mom was somewhat anti-Semitic, along with the rest of my family. Consequently, when Mom moved, my relationship with my family deteriorated to nothing for a few years. This even included my brother Jackie.

After Mom moved, Sidra increasingly pressured me to find another apartment. Her father Jack, who meant a lot to me, agreed. With his help as a cosigner, we leased an apartment at Dorilyn Terrace Apartments near Levittown. This was really a nice apartment, probably the nicest place I'd lived to that point. It even had air-conditioning. With the new apartment we had to buy furniture, with which Jack, again, helped us. Up to this point I'd had a '52 Ford, but Sidra wanted her own car, so we bought a 1961 Oldsmobile convertible. That car was only four years old, and of course, Jack helped us buy it.

Only now, in writing this, do I realize that Sidra tried to change me completely. Next came my job. Sidra was always against my working at Owens-Illinois, keeping in mind that I worked the midnight shift. It definitely hit me that a change was necessary when a friend of mine, who also worked at Owens-Illinois, was retiring at sixty-five. He received no celebration, no congratulations, just finished his shift and went home. That was the day I decided that I would find another job, even though they gave me all the overtime I could take. I worked as much as I could, because I needed to pay the bills.

Jack worked for the Veterans Administration full time and had been there for years. He also had a part-time job in the jewelry department at Two Guys. He told me of an opening in the shoe department for a manager trainee, which I applied for and got in February 1966 after one interview with Sam Capri, the department manager, and two interviews with Milt Bowder, the district manager for Morse Shoe. I accepted this job making less per hour than I did at the factory, but I saw a future. I was required to work forty-eight hours every week. The first forty hours I worked were straight time, with the next eight at half rate. I have no idea how they got away with it, because I think it was against the law. Dress code demanded I wear a tie, even though I had to unload a truck every day.

In May 1966, a new store was opening in Bethlehem, Pennsylvania, and I was asked to be the manager. Working for the district manager, Milton Bowder, I was later to find out that the only reason I was promoted was because I was thinner than Freddy, commonly referred to as Fat Freddy, even though he was far superior as a manager. Bethlehem was about an hour and a half's drive from Levittown, so instead of driving home every night, I found a room that I could rent for $25 a week.

This was about the time that Sidra and I started arguing. Consequently, instead of me coming back from Bethlehem to our apartment, I would go to her parents' home. This was the beginning of our breakup. Other than sex, our relationship was over. The end came when Sidra overheard a telephone conversation I had with Dolly. I left that relationship with nothing other than my '52 Ford.

CHAPTER 4

Morse Shoe and Jersey City

I WAS TRANSFERRED TO JERSEY City, New Jersey, a much higher volume store. Marvin Kaplan became my district manager. The rule of protocol in Morse Shoe was that if someone had a higher position, he was to be called by his surname. Marvin Kaplan became "Mr. Kaplan." Marvin Kaplan became the third of four influential and important men in my life. He dressed as if he'd just come out of a quality men's magazine, and drove an Oldsmobile Toronado. He really knew the shoe business. To try and reduce to paper what I learned from Marvin Kaplan would be harder than hard, but God, I learned a lot. He would take me to other stores to organize and clean. He would also take me to new store openings throughout New England and the Midwest, sometimes sending me on my own. There came a time when I lost my ability to register a vehicle, and he would lend me his car to drive to other stores. He also taught me how to drive a 24-foot truck. He explained: Drive straight; if you have to back up, go slow; and when you hit, you're there. It always worked.

If I thought the Kensington section of Philadelphia was tough, it was nothing next to Jersey City. It was one of the most corrupt places I'd ever been in my life. It was also filthy. It made Philadelphia look clean, even though I thought Philadelphia was the armpit of the world. The shoplifting in the Jersey City stores was unbelievable. People smoked inside the store. They drank. There was no respect for anything or anyone, and I guess now is the time to express my observation: Half the girls in Jersey City had bad teeth and put out; half the girls from Newark had bad skin and put out. By the time I left Jersey City, my accomplishments were twenty-seven. Black, white, young, old—it didn't matter.

There was a time when I was transferred to the Kearny, New Jersey, store for a few months, a cashier from the food department kept hanging around, tempting me to have sex with her, which I did, only to find out that she had a husband. I had learned a lesson when I first came to Jersey City. An older woman, maybe thirty-three years old, drove from Bethlehem to Jersey City just to have sex. She invited me to spend the weekend at her home in Bethlehem. While I was there, her estranged husband came home. Naturally, there was a fistfight. The only thing I could do was defend myself, because I knew I was wrong. That would be a mistake that I would never knowingly make again. In my opinion, married women were off-limits

Once I found out that the cashier was married, we ended our relationship. I bring this up for only one reason: She introduced me to her twin sister Sue, who wasn't married. She was really a fine-looking woman who worked full time for an insurance company in Newark, and part-time at Two Guys in Kearny. I had a great relationship with her. You might even say that I was a little in love with her. Every night she would come home with me. We would make love, and I would fall asleep. She would take my car and go home. The following morning, I would get a ride to work. One night on her way home, she was in an auto accident, and I found out she didn't have a driver's license. If I'd said she'd taken my car, she would've been charged with auto theft, so I admitted in court that I lent her my car. The judge revoked my ability to register a vehicle, which meant I was walking again.

I continued to see Sue only because we had mutual friends, and we could get rides. I know she really loved me, and she tried to pressure me into marriage, telling me she was pregnant. Thank God I'd already made a decision not to divorce Sidra until I'd found a woman I loved. Sue's last ploy was to get engaged to another guy. I think she really thought that I would break down and ask her to marry me. I didn't, so she got married. Two days after her honeymoon was over, she came to my apartment and we made love. She then informed me she got married. That was the last time I saw Sue. I learned from her sister a few years later that she had died. I still say good morning to her also.

It was in the summer of 1967 that I dated a girl who lived in Upper Montclair, New Jersey. To get to Upper Montclair from Jersey City, you had to go through Newark. In July 1967, the Newark race riots were happening. Black people were rioting in the Central Ward because of alleged police brutality, political exclusion of blacks from city government, urban renewal, inadequate housing, lack of employment, and poverty. Some local government agency was proposing moving residents from their homes in order to build a medical school/hospital complex. This involved 150 acres. The black community saw this as "Negro removal," as opposed to "urban renewal" referred to by the local government. On several occasions the National Guard, which had been stationed at intersections, would stop me from driving down a particular block and tell me that some nut was on the roof shooting. Officially, the death toll was said to be at twenty-six. I would almost guarantee the number was a lot higher. It seemed to me that Newark Bay was raised by three inches due to the deceased people disposed there.

All during 1966 and 1967, I would go back to Levittown every now and then and have sex with Sidra. We were still officially married in the fall of '67. Sidra told me she was pregnant and it was mine. I did have my doubts, because she was spending time in Florida, dancing in some kind of club. On my days off, Sidra would come with her parents to look for an apartment in North Jersey. We never found one and she decided that she wasn't moving to North Jersey.

I was informed over the phone that her daughter, Stacy, was born on March 1, 1968. I was never permitted any input regarding Stacy, even as to the choice of the name. Within a few months of her birth, Sidra took me to court to pay child support, even though I had been paying child support without a court order. Sidra would never take me to court again for anything, to her credit. My brother Jackie and his first wife, Tina, had broken up. They had a daughter, Joanne, whom Jackie regularly visited, but it was a very awkward situation. I wasn't going to create the same type of situation, so I decided that I would not try to be a strong influence in Stacy's life.

It was sometime in 1967 that I grew up, when it came to women. I was twenty. Jeanette was eighteen and a virgin. We were in bed completely nude, and I was ready, but would not because I was not in love with her. She would've been number twenty-eight.

Since I was not permitted to register a vehicle, I had to take a bus to work until I met this absolutely gorgeous Puerto Rican girl who worked in another department.

She became my ride to work and my partner in bed. I bring this up because she was finishing high school at night.

For the most part, I had nothing to do at night without an automobile, so I decided to go back and finish high school. She made it sound like a good idea. What made it a little better was that the Marine Corps was giving me money to finish school. This is when I contacted Mr. Diddo from Benjamin Franklin Junior High School for my school records. It was in September 1967 that I registered at Bayonne High School. This would turn out to be one of my best decisions of all time.

It was in early 1968 that I managed to get back my ability to register a vehicle. I made a pledge to myself that I would never lose the ability to drive or register a vehicle again. I also imposed self-discipline: I didn't buy a car. I continued to take a bus to work and to go to school at night. In September 1967, I started tenth grade. In September 1968, I started eleventh grade.

Shortly after being transferred to Jersey City, I found a fourth-floor walk-up apartment on 761 Avenue A in Bayonne. It was a few blocks from Bayonne High School. This was an old building. It even had a dumbwaiter for the trash. A dumbwaiter is a shaft with a box that you raise or lower with a rope. No one ever took the trash off of it; therefore, the dumbwaiter was always full and you had to walk your trash to the basement.

In 1966 in Bayonne, the landlords never got the apartments ready. You had to paint and clean the apartment yourself, but you had a choice as to color since you supplied the paint. With a good cleaning job and new furniture, the apartment looked great. I would stay in this apartment for the next few years, paying what I think was $95 a month. All in all, not bad. The only drawback, when I did have a vehicle, was finding parking. Sometimes you had to walk four blocks from where you parked your car to the apartment building, but this was a city. I never got to know any of my neighbors, nor did I care to.

CHAPTER 5

The Beginning of Life, With Mary

IN JANUARY 1969, I STARTED the second semester of my eleventh year. It was in Mr. Haggerty's algebra class that my life changed for the better permanently. There was this most beautiful girl sitting in my seat. The only thing I could think to say to her was, "You're sitting in my seat." This was the first time that I ever spoke to Mary. I would find out that her name was Mary Montenaro. Within one year and eight months, she would be my second and last wife. With a lot of coaching, she finally agreed to let me walk her home from school. She lived at 32nd and Broadway in a first-floor apartment with her father, Vinny; her mother, Nellie; and her sister, Josephine. My reason for attending night school was to get my high school diploma. Mary's reason was to take the necessary courses so she could become a nurse. Her job at that point was working as a secretary at the Newark FBI office.

If I thought Dolly Spor was the complete package, comparing her with Mary, Dolly would be considered more as above average. Mary looked like Jacqueline Kennedy, only better-looking. She was downright beautiful, with long, straight, black hair; eyes that danced; and the best smile I'd ever seen. Her body was a 10, and I must say I was filled with lust. She dressed impeccably. (I would later find out that her wardrobe was not extensive because she had to contribute to her household. She also came from a poor family, but everything she had was quality.) She wore great perfume and smelled like a million bucks. Frankly speaking, I didn't think I had a snowball's chance in hell of developing a relationship with this goddess.

After walking her home from school a few times, I decided my priority was to get an automobile, so I bought a 1951 Buick Roadmaster, which had a lot of problems. Consequently, I bought a 1962 Pontiac Bonneville, so now we had a

place to talk at last, because she would not go to my apartment. I was very truthful with Mary from the very beginning. I explained my marital status and where I came from. After only a few months, I realized I loved her and wanted to spend the rest of my life with her, which meant I wanted to marry her. To my surprise, she loved and wanted to marry me.

The next thing on my priority list was to get a divorce from Sidra. This wasn't going to be easy. Sidra would never allow me to divorce her, something about an insult to her. Therefore, I obtained a lawyer, Jack Stevens from Bristol, Pennsylvania, with the understanding that I would pay for the divorce, but Sidra could file. The lawyer advised me that he could never represent me again—something called "conflict of interest." I believe it was in November 1969 that the divorce was granted.

From the time I met Mary, my life kept getting better and better. The year 1969 was one of the best years of my life. On the other hand, working with Marvin was getting harder and harder, because I didn't have the commitment that I had prior to meeting Mary. It got to the point that I could no longer tolerate working in Jersey

City for Marvin Kaplan. Although Marvin was a great guy personally, working for him was unbearable. I started asking for a transfer back to Levittown for two reasons. First, I would not work for Marvin anymore, and second, Mary and I were not going to live in the Bayonne/Jersey City area. There was a manager in the Levittown store who wanted to be transferred to Northern New Jersey, to be closer to his family in Long Island, New York; that was Jack Paret.

Marvin Kaplan (seated) and the new district manager for the Levittown store, Bert Actman (standing), made a deal and traded managers. I was happy and Jack was happy. Jack and his wife, Kathy, and their newborn son would come to my apartment in Bayonne, when they were looking for a place to live, prior to their transfer. Jack and I developed a friendship that still exists today after more than forty years. Jack and Kathy could be considered the salt of the earth. I mentioned Bert Actman would be my new district manager. I had met Mr. Actman at the store opening in Bethlehem when I first became a store manager. I knew him only in passing. His first words to me, when I actually was transferred to Levittown, were that if I could do the same job Jack did, we wouldn't have any problems. This was about October 1969. Bert Actman would go on to be the fourth, and maybe in some areas the most, important man in my life. I learned so much from Bert Actman, by accident or on purpose, that I'm extremely proud to call him my mentor. At the time of this writing—April 26, 2013—I am sixty-six years old and Bert Actman is eighty-nine years old, to be ninety on May 25, and we talk at least weekly.

Mary and I would go to dinner every Saturday and Sunday. In the summer, we would go to the shore. I spent every minute that I could with her. I would get butterflies in my stomach when I was going to see her. Up to this point, my religion was Lutheran, but to see Mary more often, I would go to Mass with her every Sunday at St. Henry's (right) in Bayonne. We could walk to  Mass, it was that close. When we went to see the priest about getting married, I was informed by Father McCusker that it would be easier if I converted, since I had previously been married; fortunately, not in the Catholic Church. I then started taking lessons from Father McCusker who, ironically, was a former Marine in the Korean War. We spoke more about the Marine Corps than about the Catholic religion. We also asked Father McCusker if we should tell Mary's parents about my first marriage and Stacy. Since we were going to live about seventy miles away, he advised us not to tell them. That was a relief, because I didn't want to.

I recall the first time I was invited to a family function of Mary's family at Aunt Maggie's house. There were about forty people there. All were of dark-complexion with dark hair, except for whom I would later call Uncle Andy, and me; we were the only light-skinned, light-haired people there. I was surprised at how welcome they made me feel, and that feeling still exists today after over forty years of marriage.

Some of the people I learned to love and cherish in Mary's family were: First, her mother, Nellie (pictured next to bride), who was always kind to me and made me feel welcome. She was short, thin, and truly a humble woman, who worked at an insurance agency in Bayonne. She was a very simple and uncomplicated woman, and with the help of her daughters, kept an almost sterile house very neat and orderly. I would soon learn that her daughter Mary had the same trait. Too bad Nellie had only been in my life for about twelve years when she died of cancer at the age of fifty-four. I'm sure she sits in heaven with God, looking down and guiding Mary. Life is less without Nellie.

Second, her sister, Josephine (pictured far right), who was about three years younger than Mary and different in a kind way. Prior to my arrival and maybe a little after, Josephine was Mary's best friend. Mary loved her like no tomorrow, and if Mary loved her, then I did. You will hear more about Josephine in this writing.

Third, Mary's cousin Josephine, whom I will refer to as "Picarelli." Picarelli was my age, and she was married to Jerry Picarelli. Jerry was still in the Air Force when I met Josephine and him. They had just had a new son named Ciro. I would later go on to become Ciro's sponsor, also known as godfather. He was my second godson and third godchild. Josephine and Jerry attempted to get Mary and me to go to Marriage Encounter, claiming that would strengthen our marriage. We never went. Jerry and Josephine's marriage did not last. Picarelli will also be mentioned later in this writing.

Fourth are Mary's Uncle Andy and Aunt Carmela (pictured left). Carmela was Mary's mother's sister. Uncle Andy had a camera store in Jersey City, among other holdings. He was always there to help anyone out of a jam. He was a real stand-up guy. Aunt Carmela worked in a textile mill in Bayonne with her sister, Anna. Carmela and Anna were first-generation Italians. You could not mention Andy without Carmela and Anna. They were inseparable. Andy and Carmela became my godparents when I converted to Catholicism. To this day, I still wear the cross they gave me. When I was first transferred back to Levittown, Andy and Carmela would let me stay at their house

on Saturday night so I wouldn't have to drive back to Levittown. As with everything else, I wore out my welcome. Andy, Carmela, and Anna, I understand from Mary, were very instrumental in Mary and her sister Josephine having a normal childhood. My father-in-law never really had a decent job, and never made enough money to provide for his wife and daughters. As a matter of fact, Aunt Anna (left) and Aunt Carmela (right) took Mary to a New York City factory for her wedding dress. Any family function would not be

complete without Anna, Carmela, and Andy. Uncle Andy was not in my life that long either. He died in 1975, whereas Aunt Carmela and Aunt Anna both died early in the twenty-first century.

Fifth, Aunt Maggie, who was Mary's mother's brother's wife. She was also Picarelli's and Paula's mom. She lived at 21st and Avenue A in Bayonne. She was the widow of Mary's Uncle Paulie, who died shortly before I met Mary. Aunt Maggie was one of the most giving people that I've known, with a great sense of humor. Aunt Maggie always had a smile and a kiss and a hug for everyone, always was up, never boring or depressing. My great relationship with Aunt Maggie lasted until her death in 2013.

Sixth are Uncle Jimmy and Aunt Rae and their three sons, Sal, Ralph, and Vinny. They lived on 19th Street in the same building as Uncle Andy, Aunt Carmela, and Aunt Anna. Uncle Jimmy was Mary's mother's brother. They always made me feel welcome. Sal would go on to become a doctor. Ralph, I always felt, was going to be a professional student, but later I came to believe that he probably works for the intelligence community, although he's never admitted it. Ralph is a good guy. Vinny, I understand, lives and works in Bayonne. Uncle Jimmy passed away a few years ago, and Aunt Rae is still in my life at the time of this writing.

Seventh, the only person who showed resistance to admitting me into the family was my father-in-law-to-be Vinny. When I asked him in December 1969 if I could marry Mary, he said no. I was only being polite when I asked him. Regardless of what his answer was, I was going to marry her. That December, I gave Mary a pair of gloves with the ring on the ring finger of the left glove. The ring was a pretty big diamond, and I thought I did pretty good. A few days after Christmas, Mary informed me that she loved the ring, but when she put her finger on the one side of the ring, there was a big black mark, which was a carbon deposit. I never said I was good at picking out jewelry. I returned the ring to the store on South Street where it was purchased. Mary and I bought a nicer, but smaller, ring at Sofia's on West Side Avenue in Jersey City.

Eighth, Mary's friend Mary Lynn Hoover (maiden name, Giacobe) and her husband, Richie. They had just gotten married when I met Mary. They rented a fourth-floor walk-up apartment on 54th Street in Bayonne. They were really nice people, and both were in our wedding party. Our friendship would last until their first child was born. That was when Mary and Mary Lynn started to lose contact with one another. Unfortunately, every attempt that I've made to reconnect with them has failed, but I won't give up.

Since Mary's family had nothing saved and my family had no money, Mary and I decided, when we were sure that we were going to get married, to start saving money for our wedding. Everything I would contribute, Mary would match. Mary opened a savings account, and this is how we were going to pay for our wedding, and we did. I was surprised how much we could save. I guess now is the time to mention that Mary and I had talked about who was going to handle our finances after we were married. As I said to Mary, and I quote, "I have lived in the street many times, and if I caused us to live in the street because of my inability to handle money, I would feel real bad. But if you caused us to live in the street, it wouldn't be anything new to me, and I wouldn't be angry." So she was going to handle our finances, which was really a wise move on my part, because she did an outstanding job, and for the most part, still does.

When I first moved back to Levittown from Jersey City, my brother Walter and his wife Pat allowed me to stay at their home at 42 Rolling Lane. Basically, all I did was sleep and shower there. Every opportunity that Mary and I had, we would look for homes in Levittown. For the most part, we liked the Levittowner-type home. At that time, they were selling for about $17,000. This was above our budget, so we decided to live in the apartment for one year and save money. I'd only lived with Walter and Pat a few months when Mary and I found an apartment at 41 Joseph Place in Orangewood Park in Levittown. This complex had just been built and was very nice. The swimming pool was right behind our patio. The only thing inconvenient was that Mary had to take our clothes to the Laundromat across the parking lot. We rented the apartment for about six months. Before we got married, I would pick Mary up in Bayonne on Sundays, because I worked on Saturdays, and we would look for furnishings. Mary did great! She furnished the whole apartment for about $700.

One drawback to being transferred to Levittown was that I didn't get to see Mary that much, only on weekends, primarily because I was still going to school and having to work every Saturday. I would drive up to Bayonne on Saturday night and take Mary to dinner or a show. I  would then come up on Sunday morning, and Mary and I would go to Mass and do something for the day. The other drawback was that Mary was forced to make all the arrangements for the wedding, which she did without complaining. The wedding reception was at Hi-Hat Caterers on 54th and John F. Kennedy Boulevard in Bayonne. She arranged for Pepe Morreale and his four-piece band to play, and for Joe Bandinelli to take pictures for our wedding album.

At least two of my brothers told me that it was the best wedding they had ever been to, even though we had no cocktail hour or hors d'oeuvres. We merely had a setup, which was a bottle of liquor and soft drinks, but frankly, this was all we could afford. I must say, the wedding was a blur. All of my family showed up, except my

brothers Donny and Ted. Barbara, Ted's wife, was nine months pregnant. They lived in Albany, Georgia, where Ted was stationed as a recruiter in the United States Marine Corps. Donny never told me why he didn't show up. Our wedding party was Mary's sister Josephine, maid of honor; my brother Jackie, best man; Josephine

Picarelli and Mary Lynn Hoover, bridesmaids; with my brother Walter and Mary Lynn's husband Richie as ushers. If I must say, it was a good affair. Our wedding was September 20, 1970, at 3 o'clock on a Sunday afternoon at St. Henry's Roman Catholic Church. The priest who married us was Father Chilmark. We wanted Father McCusker to perform the ceremony, but he had become so popular in the parish that the pastor had him transferred. I guess jealousy exists everywhere.

Mary and I spent the night in a motel near the Newark airport and honeymooned the following day in Bermuda at The Reefs hotel. In 1970, September was considered off-season; therefore, for the most part, we had the entire hotel to ourselves. Other than just having a ball, four things stand out:

1. The piano player at The Reefs was a recent graduate of the Juilliard School of Music in New York City, and he played a great piano. Since the hotel was empty, for the most part, we had all of his attention.
2. On our first night in Bermuda, Mary and I decided it would be romantic to take a walk on the beach until the sand crabs chased us off.
3. We had a beautiful view of the Atlantic Ocean from our bungalow high on a cliff.

4. While on our motorbike exploring the island, we came across an abandoned military facility with a big sign at the front gate stating, "Authorized Personnel Only." Well, another couple rode up, and I told them we were authorized and they were authorized too. We both got thrown off.

It was a great beginning to our marriage.

We finally did buy a Levittowner after one year of saving and living in an apartment. We'd saved $2,000. The price of the home went up by $2,000. We stuck our necks out and paid $19,000 for our first home at 20 Spring Lane. We purchased our home FHA/VA, which was another

benefit of the Marine Corps. When we applied for the loan, there was some resistance at the bank. Therefore, I turned to my employer, Morse Shoe, and the comptroller of the company, Tony Morra, contacted the bank and our loan was approved. This is where I learned that business accounts could be used for personal benefit. After the closing was over, Mary and I had $3.46 in our savings account, but Mary and I owned our own home with a mortgage payment of about $87 a month. This included property tax. I was twenty-four, and Mary was twenty-two.

Walter lent me one of his trucks, and Mary and I moved from our apartment at 41 Joseph Place to our home at 20 Spring Lane. We weren't aware of it at the time, but my brother Jackie lived on Schoolhouse Lane, almost directly behind us, which made things a little more convenient because Jackie had the basic tools and things you needed to maintain a home. The only notable things about 20 Spring Lane were:

1. Mary and I painted the entire exterior of the home over a weekend. This was the last time Mary ever painted anything.

2. I learned how to put up a fence to keep our dogs confined. Mary and I wanted to get a dog, preferably a Great Dane. We had already picked the name for him: because we enjoyed watching Star Trek, we were going to call him "Mr. Spock." However, when we priced a Great Dane, we couldn't afford one, so we bought an Irish setter instead and named him Mr. Spock. On one of my trips to Atlantic City for Bert Actman, I hit and killed a dog in Mount Holly, New Jersey. I continued on my trip to Atlantic City, and when I came home, Mary and I took the dog to an animal shelter in Lahaska, Pennsylvania, for cremation. While we were there, we saw this beautiful Irish setter. He had everything that was right, and we adopted him. Mary and I could not figure out why someone would give up such a perfect dog (which we would name "Serge"). The first Christmas Eve at 20 Spring Lane, we rushed Serge to the animal hospital, where he was diagnosed with hip dysplasia. At that time Serge was one year old, and we were told his life would be shortened due to his disease. He lived to be twelve years old. Serge and Mr. Spock never grew out of their craziness.

3. I got to know my brother Bill better, while doing a project on our carport. My brother Bill just kind of stopped in and gave me a hand. From that point on, he would stop in occasionally, and we got to know one another as men.

4. Mary and I got to meet Ruth Durnin, Charlie's wife. Charlie was the brother of my brother Walter's wife, Pat. They lived in the Mill Creek section of Levittown. Charlie was working at U.S. Steel in Fairless Hills, Pennsylvania. Ruth worked for an insurance company in Philadelphia. At that time, they had no children. They were saving their money to build a new home, which they started right before Mary and I moved to New England. When I say they wanted to build a new home, it is exactly what they did. They bought property in Solebury Township, Pennsylvania, and Charlie actually built the house himself, with the help of his friends. To me, this was a great accomplishment, considering that Charlie was brought up in Philadelphia. Where he developed his skills, I have no idea, but he really did a good job. You will hear more about Ruth and Charlie in this writing. Ruth would go on to become one of Mary's best friends.

One of the conditions of my promotion at Morse Shoe was relocation. Early in 1974, I was promoted to district manager with the district in Upstate New York, which included Albany, Glens Falls, Schenectady, Kingston, Syracuse, and seven other cities. I would drive up on Monday and stay until Saturday. I would come home every other weekend. The weekends, I would stay in Albany. Mary would come up to look for a home. Keep in mind that I hated the cold when I was younger, and Upstate New York was very cold, and during the time we were there, the clock was not turned back in the fall season, making it very dark in the morning.

Every time Mary came up, she cried. She hated it, and that's an understatement. I guess I made things worse because I was trained to spend company money as if I were spending my own money, so I stayed in a Chinese motel, which she also hated. It came to the point that I had to speak to my regional supervisor, Edward King This was the person who trained Marvin Kaplan, I think. Marvin learned many good things, but perhaps some bad things from Edward King This man was really mean, and he lived for the company. I guess they paid him well. He had no respect for anyone or anything. He was rude. I don't think he had a personal life at all. Frankly, in my opinion he was a downright undesirable ("undesirable" is the best description that I've come up with yet to describe Edward King). I told him I was sorry, but my wife and I would not move to Upstate New York, and I was sorry because of the money the company had spent in my training. I was surprised when he told me it wasn't necessary for us to move at this time, but I might have to move in the future.

Since there was a district in Southern New Jersey and Pennsylvania that was available to me, I would be working for a new regional supervisor, Merle Pine. I had known Merle Pine from when I was first promoted to manager. I was in Bethlehem and Merle was in Allentown, Pennsylvania. As a matter of fact, I replaced Merle in Jersey City when I was first transferred there. Merle was an intelligent, happily married man. But he always seemed a little off-center, kind of nerdish. In my first district working for Merle Pine, I had stores in Northern and Southern New Jersey and Southeastern Pennsylvania. One of the stores in my first district was the Levittown store, where I had previously been the manager. This meant I would be the supervisor to managers who were previously my peers. For the most part, this was not a problem. In a few cases, I had to prove my ability.

The day I got transferred to Merle's region, I was welcome in the core of district managers, which meant I called them by their first name and had dinner with them. One of the rules of being a district manager was that you were supposed to work and eat out a few nights a week, and since there were five or six district managers in our area, we got together for dinners where I got to know these people as men, not bosses. This was just another step in my maturing, for I was only twenty-seven years old and one of the youngest district managers in Morse Shoe. Things went well, for the first year or so, until Edward King came to inform me that I would be transferred to the Fayva Division of Morse Shoe, and I would be transferred to Northern New Jersey or Southern New York. He reminded me of my failure to move to Albany when I was first promoted, about a year earlier.

Another thing that occurred while I lived in Levittown and worked for Merle Pine was the death of my father. My brothers Jackie and Donny had found my father living in Port Royal, Virginia. Prior to his death in 1974, Jackie and Donny asked me if I would like to meet him. I declined because I thought it would be disrespectful to my mother, due to the life my father had imposed on my mom, and furthermore, I would not give the bastard the satisfaction, after the childhood he'd forced on my brothers and me.

In 1974, Jackie informed me that our father, Ruben Lee Pitts, had died of a heart attack, and he wanted to know if I would like to attend the funeral services. I informed my mother that I would be going to Port Royal for his services, basically because I wanted to see if he had hair. He was sixty-eight years old. At the time of his death, he had hair. I started to lose my hair at the age of sixty-one. Getting back to the services, Jackie, Donny, and I sat in the first row, where I observed two younger girls and a very young boy. I asked my cousins, whom I had just met, who these young people were, and I was told they were my half-sisters and half-brother.

It appeared my father was also a bigamist, for he had married Idonya without benefit of divorce from my mother. She was the mother of the children who I learned were my sisters Jackie and Gail and my brother Tim. After meeting Idonya, whom I found to be very charming and a humble woman, I immediately liked her. It seemed she was not aware of my brothers and me prior to her marriage to my father. At this writing nearly forty years later, I still speak with her about once a year. Unfortunately, I haven't been able to establish a meaningful friendship with my sisters and brother.

CHAPTER 6

Connecticut and Fayva Shoe (1976–1978)

As I said before, Edward King informed me that I would be transferred to the Fayva Division of Morse Shoe in either Northern New Jersey or Southern New York. Somehow, I was transferred to Connecticut and was allowed to live anywhere I wanted, as long as it was in Southeastern Connecticut.

To this point, I'd only been to Connecticut to open, refixture, or close stores, and twice to see my Aunt Jane and Uncle Bob Harvey (pictured below). They lived in Naugatuck, Connecticut, which was about eight miles from Waterbury,

Connecticut. The first time I was in Naugatuck was for my cousin Bobby's funeral. The second time was for my Uncle Bob's funeral. Uncle Bob was my mother's older brother, and unfortunately, I never got to know him very well. It was my understanding from the people I met in Naugatuck that he must've been one great guy. I never got to know either one very well.

I learned to have my fear of diabetes because of my cousin Bobby. His diabetes cost him his marriage, eyesight, and life at a very young age. His sons Bobby and Patrick lived with their mother and stepfather, Roger, in Beacon Falls, Connecticut. Mary and I got to know

Bobby pretty well prior to his moving to California to work for the Hughes Aircraft Company, where he remained until his retirement in 2011, after he'd moved to Tucson, Arizona. We still speak every year or so. I never got to know Patrick that well. I believe he went to mechanics school and moved to Scottsdale, Arizona. I still have some of the tools that belonged to my cousin Bobby, given to me by my Aunt Jane. Bobby shared with me that his father was pretty good with tools and actually showed him and Patrick how to use tools, even after he was blinded by diabetes.

Aunt Jane and Uncle Bob met in Philadelphia in the early 1900s. I understand my Uncle Bob was completely taken by Aunt Jane, but there was one problem: my Uncle Bob was German Protestant and Aunt Jane was Italian Catholic. In the early 1900s, Italians were really looked down upon, so my grandmother and grandfather were not too thrilled at the prospect of having a WOP (which meant an Italian "With Out Papers") and Catholic, no less, in their family. Aunt Jane told Mary and me that my grandmother attended their wedding in a housedress to show her disapproval of having a first-generation Italian in their family.

Aunt Jane lived with her mother and father prior to their wedding in Philadelphia. Right after the wedding, Aunt Jane's parents moved back to Naugatuck, where they were from originally. After the wedding, my grandparents were so hard on Aunt Jane and Uncle Bob that they also moved to Naugatuck and made a life of their own. They made a good life for themselves.

Getting back to my transfer: Not knowing Connecticut very well, it was going to take time for Mary and me to find a home. After visiting Aunt Jane and realizing that she was struggling financially, I first asked the person in Morse Shoe who approved expense accounts, Jimmy Johnson, if I could pay Aunt Jane a weekly amount to cover room and board. My thinking was that it would be good for me and good for Aunt Jane as well. I was really surprised when he agreed, with no problem. I later learned that I could go to Jimmy with any problem, and he would help me with a favorable decision. You could refer to Jimmy as my "rabbi." I still speak with him about twice a year. I then asked Aunt Jane if that arrangement would work for her, and she became very excited at the prospect of having my company. This arrangement existed for about four months. In that time, Mary would come up on weekends or whenever she had the opportunity, and we would look for a home.

This is where the relationship between Mary and Aunt Jane (pictured together) really started to develop. This was also about the time Mary's mother, Nellie, started to be really sick.

We must've looked at one hundred homes in many different communities. Nothing seemed to please us until we found a house in Beacon Falls at 177 Cedar Lane, at the end of a cul-de-sac and at the top of what I considered a mountain, a mostly wooded two-acre property. The $36,000 asking price was right in our ballpark, so in early 1976 Mary and I moved to Beacon Falls with our two dogs, Mr. Spock and Serge.

The first thing I did was cut a hole through the concrete wall in the garage to build an entrance to the run I'd built below the deck. The house was a two-bedroom with one and a half baths, a dining room, a living room, a kitchen, a two-car garage under the house, and a substantial-size deck with a great view. To our surprise, the first spring several different perennial flowers bloomed. Mary and I loved this house. It was commonly known as a rancher.

I failed to mention earlier that after Mary and I got married, she got a job at Virnelson's Bakery in Andalusia, Pennsylvania. This was a family-owned business, and Mary wasn't really happy there. She resigned and got a job at Strescon Industries in Morrisville, Pennsylvania, as an executive secretary working for a man that I still would like to know today but don't, Harlan Kahler. I also failed to mention that when I met Mary, she didn't have her driver's license, so the first thing we did was to get her a driver's permit, and I taught her to drive. Edna Starroff, my cashier from Two Guys, took her for her test because I still had a Pennsylvania driver's license. She passed the first time out. (Edna is seated next to Marvin Kaplan in the picture on page 52.)

When we first got married, Aunt Anna gave us her 1956 Chevy Bel Air four-door sedan, along with other wedding gifts. It was Mary's car to drive for the next six years. When we first got the '56 Chevy, it wouldn't go over forty miles an hour. With my not having any ability as an automobile mechanic, we paid a lot to get it running correctly. Speaking of my ability as an automobile mechanic, I can take an automobile that runs poorly, tune it up, and it doesn't run at all. At the time of this writing, July 2013, we still have that '56 Chevrolet. We've been through paint jobs, motors, and interiors. We still get compliments because of its age and the color: pearl white and candy-apple green. It is still slow, even though it has a 265 V-8 engine.

When we first moved to Connecticut, my cousin Bobby Harvey introduced Mary and me to Peter Christiansen. Peter was a rotund twenty-year-old bundle of laughs, who loved Beacon Falls. The last time I spoke with Peter wasn't more than a few years ago, and he still lived in Beacon Falls and he is still big. Peter had a 1967 Dodge convertible, which he sold to Mary and me. For the life of me, I don't know why we bought it. That was Mary's car for the next two years. The '56 at this point was retired. The Dodge only lasted for two years—the two years we were in Connecticut.

On our property at 177 Cedar Lane, Mary was in the only accident she's ever had. Our driveway was gravel on a hill, and during the fall of 1976, with all the leaves on the driveway, she literally slid off the driveway onto rocks, with two tires off the ground. I had to cut trees down so that I could get the car out of the woods. Our 1974 Cutlass would never be the same. When she first had the accident, I wasn't home. She didn't get hurt. She knocked on the neighbor's door, and the man

of the house and one of his sons came over to help Mary out. They were there for fifteen minutes, according to Mary, before the wife called and told them it was time for dinner. They left and didn't return.

At that point, Mary and I learned that we were not Swamp Yankees. We were outsiders in Beacon Falls because we hadn't been born and raised there. Shortly after Mary's accident, those people moved. We were very happy because the principal of the local elementary school bought the house. He was also an outsider. I understand that he was never accepted either. We developed a great relationship, and he helped me write something for the Morse Shoe Company paper, which I quote:

"I believe an employee, regardless of rank or degree of responsibility, must make total commitment to the service. It is the employee's responsibility to ensure maximum productivity at minimum cost, while simultaneously maintaining a high level of ethical and moral standards."

Living in the woods was something new for us. I recall a time when Mary bought me a chain saw, and I decided I was going to clean up the woods. I cut up all the branches and limbs that were down and stacked them in a nice pile. Some of the smaller stuff I used to start a fire. Things were going well until a little fire broke out about twenty feet from me. Then two more fires broke out thirty to forty feet from me. Within a half hour, I had about twelve fires going. I was scared I might burn down our house. Needless to say, I got a hose and put out all my fires. It seems that some of the roots had caught fire, and that's why the fire had spread. I told myself I would never do that again, and I haven't.

I was surprised when I found out that Jack Paret and his family lived in Naugatuck. Jack had been promoted to the position of district manager about a year before me. Also, he and Kathy had recently bought a new house, which appeared to me to be on a big rock at the top of what I considered a mountain. He would later buy a house downtown, which really had charm. Jack now had one boy and two girls, and as most people who know retail know, it does not pay well. So in my opinion, he was always chasing money, though he had been paid more than most in retail. It still sucked. Jack really liked working for Morse Shoe in the discount division.

The Fayva Shoe Division, as I would soon learn, was much different than the Discount Division of Morse Shoe, which all my experience had been in. The basic concept of the Discount Division was to rent space in larger department stores, with shoes displayed on tables and racks where customers could make their selections and pay at the cash register within the shoe department. Whereas in the Fayva Division, Morse Shoe rented stores in malls and strip centers, shoes were displayed on racks, with backup inventory in the stockroom. The managers were responsible for all facets of running the store, which included hiring, developing and, if necessary, terminating employees. It was the manager's responsibility to make sure that the store opened on time and closed at the correct time, and to manage inventory control. Managers were also responsible for housekeeping on the interior, which included the restrooms and exterior of the store, and in most stores, trimming of the front window (displaying shoes for the maximum appeal).

It was my opinion after meeting the managers in my new district that they did not possess the same loyalty as managers in the Discount Division. The phrase that influenced my opinion was "this company" rather than "the company." It seemed to me that this was not unique to my district, after having worked in both the Discount and Fayva Divisions. It also seemed to me that the Fayva Division was much more expensive to operate. Morse Shoe was an old company, which had started in the Boston area with conventional shoe stores, when they developed the Discount Division. The profit increased considerably. The Fayva Division was much less profitable, in my opinion (I had learned how to read the profit and loss statement, by store, that I received monthly), and that is the reason that Morse Shoe went out of business. That, coupled with junk bonds which were purchased by the new president of the company.

Sam Albert was my first regional supervisor in the Fayva Division. He was one of the regional supervisors in the Fayva Division at that time. I had known him from when he was a district manager in the Discount Division. When I worked for Marvin Kaplan, there was no love lost between Sam Albert and Marvin Kaplan. Marvin always believed that Sam was self-centered and would always try to look like a hero at everyone else's expense. Good things, he took credit for; mistakes and screw-ups were always someone else's fault according to Marvin. I believe that Edward King trained Sam Albert, and that's why Sam was so undesirable, in my opinion.

I went into this new position with a positive attitude. Sam very shortly showed me things were not going to be that positive. I am a Catholic, and in my religion to hate is a sin, but I hated this man. He dressed with good clothes and shoes, but always looked like a schlep. His head was so far up his backside, I don't think he could breathe. He walked like a jerk, but in my opinion he thought he walked on water. Initially, I misinterpreted his rudeness. I was giving him the benefit of the doubt. He would attempt to humiliate me because I would not kiss his backside. Initially, I took his abuse, but I learned to go back at him just as hard as I could, almost bringing him to the point of losing his head and yelling.

I was required as a district manager to drive my regional manager around my district. I hated this man so much that I bought an automobile with no air conditioning just so he would not ride with me. Frankly, he made me sick to my stomach, which ultimately affected my home life. I never had the opportunity to improve things as I wanted to. I was constantly being transferred from fourteen stores to thirty-one stores to ten stores in different locations. It came to the point that I called Edward King and told him that I would not work for Sam Albert and there were four options: I could be transferred. He could be transferred. I could live with things the way they were. I could quit.

Here again I was surprised when he told me I could be transferred to Southern New Jersey (the district manager in that area wanted to be transferred to Florida, where there was an opening). Southern New Jersey at that point had a new regional supervisor, Al Martin, and that's who I would be working for. It took almost a year for me to be transferred and to move.

My conversation with Edward King was sometime around the beginning of May 1977. I remember that time because on May 12, we had snow flurries in front of my house. In my opinion, this was a sign from God that I had to get out of Connecticut by the end of summer. Our house was ready to put on the market. It was sold immediately, with closing at the end of December. The transfer to Southern New Jersey had not been completed; consequently, we asked Aunt Jane if we might live with her until we found a house in Southern New Jersey, to which she happily said yes. We put our furniture into storage and our dogs, Mr. Spock and Serge, in a long-term kennel. Aunt Jane wasn't fond of the dogs.

I recall while living at Aunt Jane's, I was scheduled to do an inventory in Newburgh, New York. It was my procedure to start the inventory the night before, which I did. I checked into a motel and planned to finish the inventory in the morning. Ironically, on the morning of the inventory, it had been snowing all night. The snowstorm was known as the Blizzard of '78. It took me only fifteen minutes longer to drive the seventy-five miles to Naugatuck, because no one was on the road. I got stuck at the bottom of the hill when we received thirty-three inches on top of the twenty-four inches that were already there. The governor of the state of Connecticut closed the state to traffic for three days. In this time, I got so bored that I used Aunt Jane's snow-blower to blow a path to her toolshed that you could've driven a Mack truck down. There was nothing in the toolshed. I then decided I would blow off every sidewalk on the block, which I did. This annoyed Aunt Jane. It was her opinion that my Uncle Bob had always done things like that for the neighbors and they'd never reciprocated the favor. I learned a very important lesson that gratitude ends with "Thank you." To expect more, you leave yourself open to disappointment.

A few weeks later, while Mary and I were in the bedroom sleeping at about 11 p.m., Aunt Jane knocked on the door. Aunt Jane never knocked on the door. When I opened the door, Aunt Jane was standing with her face full of blood. She'd been washing clothes in the basement, and when she came up the stairs, she fell. The closest hospital was in Waterbury. So I decided it would be faster if I just drove her to the hospital instead of waiting for an ambulance. I remember telling Aunt Jane to keep the towel over her face because the blood was making me sick. When we got to the hospital, I was told she'd broken her nose and had lacerations around the eyes. She looked like something from a horror show for the next three to four weeks.

I failed to mention it earlier, but right before we sold our house in Beacon Falls, Mary told me she was pregnant. At first, I was somewhat shocked. But the more I thought of it, the better I liked it. When I returned from the hospital with Aunt Jane, I got back into bed. Mary shook me and told me she was having pain. I drove her to the hospital in Waterbury. When the doctor came out after looking after Mary, he informed me we'd had a miscarriage. He told me that nature had a way of dealing with things that were less than perfect. I didn't believe it then, and I still don't believe him now. The only thing I know for sure is that it broke Mary's heart and my heart. Mary would never get pregnant again. When we first got married, we talked of having a child in three years. Three became five, and then it was not talked about anymore. Part of me regrets that Mary and I are childless, but the other part is happy. So, I really don't know.

In the time we lived in Connecticut, Mary's sister Josephine got engaged and married Bruce Nobile. Mary was in her wedding party as her maid of honor. This is about the time Mary got brave, because she started to drive to Bayonne for the preparations for her sister's wedding. Josephine and Bruce followed our lead. They made their own wedding. It was a better wedding than ours, but they had dated longer. Also, the health of my mother-in-law Nellie was deteriorating, and Mary was well aware that it was just a matter of time.

It was also in this time that I developed prostate problems. Connecticut truly wasn't good for Mary and me.

Mary and I would spend every weekend driving to Southern New Jersey. It seemed that living in the Burlington, New Jersey, area would be really centered in the district that I would be getting. So with the help of my brother Stanley's wife, Marge, we found this  three-bedroom Cape Cod-design house on Sycamore Drive in Burlington Township. The price was also right, somewhere around $36,000. We negotiated the deal with the seller, and I then went to Burlington Savings Bank in Burlington City with hat in hand to ask them for a loan. We got a fifteen-year mortgage amortized over thirty years, with a balloon payment after fifteen. I calculated that if I paid an additional $50 a month, the house would be paid for in fifteen years, completely. I found it amazingly easy to do these things on my own. Within four weeks, we'd made a deal and agreed on a closing date. From the time we first looked at the house until we moved in was five weeks. I never thought it could be done that quickly. The woman who formerly owned the house had died, and her children sold us the house.

In May 1978 the dogs, Mary, and I moved to Burlington. I met my new regional supervisor, Al Martin, and my store managers in New Jersey. Al Martin had a different management style than most people in Morse Shoe. He was hired into the company as a district manager with the understanding that he would become a regional supervisor. He had formerly been a regional supervisor for Johnston & Murphy Shoe Company. His ideas did not coincide with the ideas of Morse Shoe. I could tell within a few hours of talking with him that he was a gentleman. Working with him was like a breath of fresh air after working with Sam Albert. I was devastated when, in August, he told me he had submitted his resignation. Since he was one of the only other regional supervisors in the Fayva Division of Morse Shoe it meant that Sam Albert would be my regional supervisor again. When this was confirmed by Jimmy Johnson in the home office, I submitted my two-week notice. Edward King came and spoke with me, but my mind was made up. I would not work for Sam Albert again. So right after Labor Day week, I left Morse Shoe. (Labor Day week is one of the busiest weeks in the shoe business.)

Sam Albert made very clear his dislike for me when he told me to leave my company car parked at a store and to give the keys to the store manager. I would speak with Sam Albert one more time. After several years of not working for Morse Shoe, I was really lost. I think because that was my first real job, and I had been with them for twelve years. I called Jimmy Johnson and told him I was interested in working for Morse Shoe. There was a new regional supervisor in Southern New Jersey. I never got to speak with him, but instead, I had to meet with Sam Albert, who arranged that I meet him in the Newark airport in the middle of the night. I think he just wanted to see me grovel. He offered me a job in Baton Rouge, Louisiana, which, naturally, I declined. I'm glad I did, because it forced me to take another career direction.

I could afford to be unemployed because when we first moved back to Southern New Jersey, Mary had gotten a job with the Lincoln Property Company in Marlton, New Jersey, as an executive secretary working for Nancy Stack. Nancy Stack was a partner in the Marlton operations. She was originally from Dallas, Texas. I understand that in order to get her job originally in Dallas, she told Trammell Crow, the controlling partner in Lincoln Property Company, that she would work for nothing for a month. She did and she was hired. She advanced to become a limited partner, not only in Marlton, but in other sites as well. Mary was paid well as an executive secretary, which meant that we could afford to live on her salary for quite some time.

When I left Morse Shoe, I wanted to start a construction business. So with my nephew Michael Hansell, we went into business. It didn't go well, mainly because I had no idea how to estimate jobs, or even do a lot of jobs, and it didn't last very long.

Within the next year and a half, I had three different jobs:

1. Vista shoe company. This was a local company with stores in the Philadelphia area.

2. RG Barry shoe company. This company was the maker of Mushrooms, according to my wife. They were the most comfortable shoes yet. One of the principals in this company was a person by the name of Stands. He was a young fellow who taught me one thing, and to this day I still use it: It's nice to be important, but more important to be nice.

3. Things Remembered novelty company. The politics in this company were outrageous. Everyone, it appeared, was tearing apart everyone else in order to advance. It reminded me of a company full of SAM ALBERTs. Considering the traveling and the politics, I didn't last very long at all.

All three positions were obtained through a headhunter (a headhunter is a person who attempts to unite companies with employees). All three companies paid the headhunter. They wasted their money.

It was sometime in 1980 that Al Martin, my former regional supervisor at Morse Shoe, contacted me to see if I would be interested in being a partner in his business. He had opened two shoe stores by the name of Shoe Stop, using the Fayva shoe-store concept, in Mantua and Glassboro, New Jersey. Neither store did very well, but after my interview with Sam Albert, I would've done anything. So, I told Al Martin that I would work for free for my interest in the company. Basically, he ran the store in Mantua and I ran the store in Glassboro. I would spend one day a week in Mantua doing paperwork.

Al had a lot of good ideas and some real bad ones as well. I was under the impression that he could buy shoes. What I mean by "buy shoes" is pick shoes that could sell next season. He could pick shoes better than I, but he wasn't great at it.

Neither one of us had any concept of capitalization of a business, because we were grossly undercapitalized, which affected our cash flow, which affected our credit, which affected our ability to buy shoes at the right price to make a reasonable profit.

For the year and a half I worked with Al, I learned a whole lot about how businesses ran, what to do, and what not to do. What not to do was have his wife and children in the business. It only created problems. Also, there was no way that his family could not be paid. They needed the money. They had no Mary to fall back on. In my opinion, between Al, his wife, and his daughter, they took too much money out of the business. As I said about being undercapitalized, Al wanted to open more stores, which we did—one in Hammonton and another in Brooklawn, New Jersey.

Our credit became so poor that our vendors wanted to be paid COD. Naturally, we didn't have the money for that. After a few exceptionally bad months, Al informed me that he wanted to close the stores. I was shocked when we started running "going out of business" sales. We didn't pay our vendors. And worse, his mother had signed a note with the Small Business Administration. I believe the number was $40,000. When we didn't pay that note, his mother had to. It goes without saying that during that year and a half, I didn't receive a nickel, but I did receive knowledge, which was much more important, in my opinion. Al had no concept of money. I was convinced he was a weak businessman with no heart. Thank God I had no obligation or debt. Little did I know that when we closed the stores, I would also be closing my career in retail.

The only thing notable in the time I worked with Al was the death of my mother-in-law, Nellie. She succumbed to cancer, at age fifty-four, which she had fought for several years. My father-in-law; Mary's aunts Carmela, Anna, and Maggie; and Mary's cousins Josephine Picarelli and Paula were very helpful to Nellie at the end. Thank God Mary and I didn't settle in Bayonne, as I'm sure there's something in the air, with all the refineries and chemical factories. It's a wonder anyone lives. Tragically, Mary's sister Josephine lived in Bayonne a little longer than Mary, to complete college. After her marriage, she lived a few years in Elizabeth, New Jersey. She also died of cancer, at the age of fifty-seven, in 2010.

It was in 1978 at my first meeting with the managers in my district that I met Ed VanSciver. During the time I worked for Morse Shoe, the unwritten company rules frowned upon district managers and managers socializing. But when I left Morse Shoe, Ed contacted me and we developed a strong friendship that would last until his death in 2003. When I first met Ed in the Lawnside, New Jersey, Fayva shoe store, he was wearing trousers that I considered to be high-water trousers (high-water trousers were trousers that were too short). The Lawnside store had

sewage problems and it always smelled, no matter how much deodorant or scented spray was used, and sometimes it actually backed up. Maybe that's why Ed was wearing high-waters. I'm sure the smell prevented the Lawnside store from doing its potential volume in sales.

It was shortly after I met Ed, no more than one month, that he told me that his ex-wife had dropped his three sons and their clothing at the doorstep of the house he shared with his girlfriend, Eileen. I think Tommy was ten, Eddie was seven, and Jeffrey was five. Ed's girlfriend wanted nothing to do with Ed's sons, so Ed had to find an apartment with his boys, and in my opinion, these three boys were like wild animals. Ed's ex-wife, instead of bringing her children up, drugged them up. They had no social graces whatsoever, at least two of them still wet the bed, and Ed tried to make a bad situation good. In the short time that Ed continued to work for me, I extended every consideration possible to help him with his personal problems, and Ed never forgot it. Ed will be mentioned many times in this writing.

CHAPTER 7

First Career Change

AFTER THE SHOE STOP STORES closed, I took a few interviews with other retail companies. I did receive some offers, but I think I'd had it with retail. Mary, being aware of this, suggested I meet with a former coworker of hers, Harry Bagot. This would be a decision I would never regret. Harry had left Lincoln Property Company to work for another property management company. Harry was hired as vice president in charge of operations. I met Harry at 7 a.m. at Olga's Diner on Route 73. After being in retail, where the start time was nine or ten, it was like getting up in the middle of the night. Harry and I then drove to Atlantic City, where Harry was considering making me the property manager for five properties. I interviewed with Harry and Jack Richards, and was hired with absolutely no experience. This was the beginning of a friendship with Harry that would last to this day. Harry would grow to be one of my best friends.

All five properties were subsidized by the Department of Housing and Urban Development, referred to after this as HUD. These properties were really in bad shape; the physical condition was deplorable. They didn't seem to have enough money to pay their bills, which complicated every aspect of the property operation, as I would find out for a number of different reasons; for example, getting a rent increase. You had to petition HUD for approval, which the people working for Jack Richards were neglectful of doing.

Jack Richards was hired by Alan Levine, the owner and general partner in all the properties. Al Levine was a hell of a nice guy, but he didn't want anything to do with management, so he allowed Jack Richards to run the management company. Looking back now, Jack Richards did just about everything wrong, starting with moving from a paid office building in Pleasantville to buying a building in Cherry Hill at top dollar.

The management company had an in-house computer system, which Jack Richards decided was smarter to move outside. This mistake cost Jack Richards his job, because he failed to run parallel systems and damn near bankrupted the company. Thank God, Al Levine had deep pockets and could carry the load.

One of the memorable things about working for the management company after being promoted to having fourteen properties in my portfolio was the rehab of the property known as Elizabeth Commons, in Elizabeth, New Jersey. There were six buildings, with sixty units per building. Our task was to completely empty a building, whereas the contractor could rehabilitate and modify one building at a time. Elizabeth Commons was in the upscale area of Elizabeth. The property suffered from deferred maintenance and had a multitude of problems. There were one-, two-, and three-bedroom units. The buildings were going to be modified to have more two-bedroom and fewer one- and three-bedroom units. This decision by the powers that be would create all kinds of problems.

For the most part, the residents of the buildings were minorities, and they had bigger families. And if they made too much money, they would not be brought back to the property, after the rehab, because it was going to be subsidized, and they would not qualify for subsidies. That, coupled with the modifications in the buildings, made the job almost impossible. The management company was responsible for paying reasonable moving expenses, and for those people who were not coming back, they were obligated to pay up to $3,000 to help them get a start elsewhere. For many of the people this was not enough money, in most people's opinion, and they resisted.

There was one fellow in the A building, Mr. O., who would not leave the building, claiming that his wife had died there and there were too many memories. It took a lot of coaxing and cajoling, and a little more money, but he moved.

While this rehab was going on at Elizabeth Commons, Jack Richards was fired by Al Levine, and Jack hired Harry Bagot from the management company. Since I liked working with Harry, I decided I would go with Jack Richards and Harry. I would pay dearly for this decision later on, because the new president of the management company, Tom Hemingway, would just about blackball me from ever again doing business with the management company.

During the time I worked for the management company, one of the noteworthy things that occurred was my relationship with Mary's cousin Josephine Picarelli (the cousin who was in our wedding): it blossomed. When the Elizabeth Commons property in Elizabeth started the rehab, we needed a manager, and since Josephine was unemployed at that time, I offered her the job as manager, though she had no experience in property management. She was extremely smart and picked up things real quick. Josephine was one of those dependable people you could always count on, and frankly, she never let me down. She had a great relationship with residents, staff, and home office, and I learned to respect and love her, and I know the feeling was mutual.

Another person who worked with us at Elizabeth Commons was Lori Eberhardt. She'd formerly worked for me at Things Remembered, and I knew that she was not happy working there. Again, she had no experience in property management, but she was smart and learned things quickly. She and Josephine made a good team. I don't think we could've done better than Josephine and Lori at Elizabeth Commons. Unfortunately, Josephine and Jerry Picarelli were divorced. Josephine was totally committed to her children—Ciro, Michelle, and Paulette—and she wasn't looking for romantic involvement with anyone. On the other hand, Lori was young, never married, and had no relationship when I recruited her to work with Josephine at Elizabeth Commons I had a friend by the name of Lee Brown who worked at HUD. In my opinion, Lori and Lee were absolutely made for one another. I introduced them, and within a few years they were married. I played Cupid well.

The last person from Elizabeth Commons was Alan Levine's son, Ben. It seemed that his father wanted him to be involved in the business. So every time I went to Elizabeth Commons, which was about sixty-five miles away, Ben would drive to my house and he would go with me. He had a great sense of humor, but had no desire to be in property management. When I left the management company, Ben left as well.

The first thing I enjoyed about working in property management was that I didn't have to work on Saturdays. Quite the opposite of retail, where I had to work every Saturday. Having Saturdays free opened a whole new world of possibilities for me.

I mentioned earlier that I continued to have a friendship with Ed VanSciver from Fayva Shoe. A few months after I left Morse Shoe, Ed left Morse Shoe. I'm not sure why, but I know he was unemployed. So when a position opened in my region with the management company, I hired Ed. In my opinion, management is management. Whether you're selling shoes, selling cars, or renting apartments, management is management. Ed was also intelligent, so he did real well immediately. Fortunately for me, Ed's experience had always been in retail. So having Saturdays off was different for him as well.

I mention this because Ed and I decided to help one another with different projects. We sided the front of his house and put on a new roof. Ed was so grateful that he volunteered to bring his three sons—Tommy, Eddie, and Jeffrey—to work with me on Saturdays at the home of my former father-in-law, Jack Newberg, in Levittown. As I said earlier, I'd learned to love Jack Newberg, coupled with the fact that Jackie and I had started pouring a patio for him, but had never finished, many years earlier. I thought it would be a good idea if I sided his home in Levittown, which I did with the help of Ed and his three sons. All of us really enjoyed ourselves, and it only took about two months of Saturdays.

Working at Jack's was somewhat awkward initially, because I really didn't know how Shirley, my former mother-in-law, would receive me. More importantly, my ex-wife, Sidra, and fourteen-year-old Stacy would spend time at Jack and Shirley's. All my concerns were put to rest when Sidra and Stacy basically ignored me. I was happy about that, for there was no love lost between Sidra and me.

I was pleasantly surprised when Shirley started to develop a real like and respect for me. She was genuinely kind to us, and she even took to cooking for us. Jack, on the other hand, if I had not known better, treated me as if I were still his son-in-law, not former son-in-law. I know that man loved me as much as any father could love a son, and I loved him as much as any son could love a father.

It didn't take me long to complete all the Saturday projects that I could possibly think of. So based on Mary's suggestion, I applied to Lincoln Property Company for a job working on Saturdays. At that time, Lincoln Property was building new homes, and I was hired as a pre-title inspector. I really enjoyed myself at that job. I would lie on the floor to inspect ceilings and walls. Everything had to work perfectly. Doors had to be adjusted; touch-ups of drywall and paint were required. It really was an all-around good job. I didn't make very much money, but enjoyed myself. As a matter of fact, I was called "Harvey Saturday." Little, at that time, did I realize that I was perfecting some of the talents I would use extensively later on.

As I said earlier, after leaving the management company, I went to work with Harry Bagot and Jack Richards. The company that Jack Richards established was Langhorne Properties, Incorporated. The home office was literally in his home in Langhorne, Pennsylvania. My office was at one of the properties. Now is the time to explain how Jack Richards established this company. He literally took accounts from the management company, to the best of my knowledge. There were three or four different properties, with each property paying about $84,000 a year in management fees for an average 100-unit property. This, coupled with a relationship developed while working for the management company with George Grossman, a syndicator selling tax shelters in real estate, while maintaining a controlling-interest partner in each deal. (Jack Richards developed this relationship while working for the management company; therefore, the relationship should have stayed with the management company, in my opinion.)

My first assignment with Langhorne Properties was two properties in New Jersey. These properties owed money to everybody in America, it appeared. When I called to order from our vendors, they would laugh right before they told me it was COD. I managed to get their fiscal position straightened out. This was due to rent increases in the amount of 60 percent or greater two years running. I must reiterate that while these properties were with the management company, there had not been a rent increase in approximately eight years. Shame on the management company, or as I look at it now, shame on Jack Richards.

Harry's position with Langhorne Properties was to seek out deals for George Grossman, which Harry was quite successful at. My position was operations. With the ever-increasing deals with George Grossman, we had properties that we managed in Chicago, Indianapolis, Boston, New Haven, and Philadelphia, with several in New Jersey. One of the greatest advantages of working with Jack Richards was that he left you alone, and I ran the properties. Anyway, I saw, for the most part, that the properties were easy to get under control. But there always seemed to be a problem with money. Based on my calculations of chargeable expenses, this should not have been. This was the reason I started to scrutinize all expenses, and I was shocked to find that many, many expenses were charged to the property that, in my opinion, were not the responsibility of the property to pay. Again in my opinion, we were up to the line on right or wrong, and frankly, I think we went over the line several times.

I first brought this to Harry's attention, and I don't think he was totally surprised, because he had his own suspicions. So both Harry and I brought this to Jack Richards's attention. Jack Richards blew it off as if it were no big deal. Both Harry and I knew that it was a big deal and were concerned that the Inspector General's office or *60 Minutes* would be at our office one day. We had heard horror stories of companies and individuals who didn't play by the rules. Their punishment was severe.

An example of this arose shortly after Jack Richards had been in business about six months. Jack Richards moved to Cranston, Rhode Island, and worked out of his house. We opened an office in Clementon, New Jersey, furnished with funds primarily from the properties we managed. After repeatedly talking to Jack Richards about this problem, Harry and I decided to commit mutiny. We decided to contact all of our property owners and tell them about our suspicions. Some of the property owners wanted to go with Harry and me, but most wanted to stay with Langhorne Properties, so Harry and I opened an office in Harry's house in Westmont, New Jersey. Try as we might, we could not make enough money to support both of us. So Harry and I made a deal with Jack Richards that we would go back to work for Langhorne Properties only if we had the checkbooks for the properties. Jack Richards agreed to this and, in fact, gave me a raise in 1984. I was making $70,000 a year—not bad for a kid from the projects in Southwest Philly.

We opened an office in Mount Laurel, New Jersey. Harry and I had only been gone about five months when we came back. It took us about a year to straighten out the compliance problems that were created while we were gone. The paperwork mess was so bad that I bought a computer. Computers were relatively new at that point. I hired a programmer to write a program for a general-ledger system, which was required by our property owners and HUD. I went as far as to hire my ex-wife's father, Jack Newberg, to be the input person to bring us into compliance within our contractual agreements. It was a true joy working with Jack for those few months. Things seemed to be going very well for about two years, when Jack decided that he wanted the checkbooks with him in Rhode Island. I promptly gave a two-month notice and left Langhorne Properties. I didn't want to go to jail.

Langhorne Properties lasted another two years. As I understand it, their main property owner, George Grossman, filed legal action against Jack Richards and won,

which drove Langhorne Properties out of business. During the time I worked with Jack Richards, I really had an opportunity to go further in depth with the operation of business, for which I am truly thankful now.

The only thing I regret that happened during the time I worked for Jack Richards is that my mother (left) died after fighting cancer for many years. Cancer did not kill her though. She never wanted to go into a nursing home, but frankly, after her last hospitalization, there were no alternatives. She was more than my sister Sophia could handle on her own, and I do believe Mom gave up. She only lasted a few days in the nursing home. I've never stopped missing her.

Mom was born in June 1908 and died in March 1985, making her seventy-six years old at the time of her death. This, by far, was the most tragic thing that had happened in my life. As a matter of fact, I started saying good morning to my mom every day, knowing it would keep her memory alive. Somehow it made me feel better or closer to her. I then started saying good morning to all the people I knew who had passed

away. At this writing in October 2014, I say good morning to over four hundred people every day. I affectionately call this my "morning club."

The last time Mom hit me, I was thirty-five years old. The only thing I could say to her was, "Mom, did you have to hit me in front of my wife?" Of course, I deserved to be hit, in her eyes, because I used my favorite word in front of her. It begins with F and ends with K. I think you can understand.

CHAPTER 8

Kruger Limited Corp.

IT WAS AUGUST 22, 1985, when I got the corporate name Kruger Limited Corp. from the State of New Jersey. I got the idea for the name from the TV miniseries *Master of the Game.* It was a story about a Scotsman who, with the help of a black man in South Africa, robbed a diamond mine. They penetrated the diamond mine from a sandy shore. One of the guard dogs that was held back, probably because the guards were too lazy to make the effort to capture the thieves, was named Kruger. Both men went on to be extremely successful.

On that day, I opened a checking account with Burlington Savings Bank. I also got cards made and obtained insurance. I was ready for business. I had filed for the name through my accountant, Simeon, a few weeks before August 22. Simeon had been doing Mary's and my taxes for years prior to 1985. To this date, October 2013, Simeon is still my accountant. He is conservative and has definitely kept me out of trouble.

I was fortunate I went into business when I did. My first customer was Capital Site Management. In some of the properties that I had formerly managed, initially I did anything I could to make money. This included painting drywall, flooring, carpentry, and so on. I managed to hire three people within the first weeks of September 1985. I sold my 1984 Cougar automobile and bought a 1985 Ford F-150 pickup truck.

My first big job was in West Haven, Connecticut, installing metal capping and soffits over wood on porches. The job was broken down into three sections. The final section was done in November 1985. I had arranged with Aunt Jane that my crew and I could spend the nights that we were in West Haven at her home, now in Waterbury, which is only a few miles from West Haven. On the last night we spent there, when I woke up in the morning, Aunt Jane told me she didn't feel well.

I suggested that she take it easy that day, and definitely turn the heat up. That day was the last day that we would be working in New Haven. When we finished for the day, my crew and I came back to New Jersey. When I got home, Mary told me that Aunt Jane had been taken to the hospital. After she had been in the hospital a few days, I was told by her sister-in-law, Mary, that Aunt Jane was terminal. I spoke to Aunt Jane one more time, knowing that she was in pain. I told her not to fight it, that she should join her husband and son, whom she always talked about. She died a few hours later.

When Mary and I had left Connecticut seven years earlier, Aunt Jane was having really severe financial problems. I told her, in my opinion, she should sell her house—a house that had been totally paid for—and rent an apartment. She would then have the money to travel to see her grandsons and, frankly, do some of the things that she'd always wanted to do. Ironically, when she passed away, she was almost broke. There was one incident that alarms me to this day. When her grandsons came in from Arizona, they called me and asked if I had taken the insurance policies. I felt like a thief. They never even bothered to call later to say that they had found them. I forgave them, considering that they'd had a hard time finding those insurance policies.

At this point two of the four most important women in my life were gone: Mom and Aunt Jane. At this writing in October 2013, thank God Mary, the love of my life, and my sister Sophia are still very much a part of my life.

I quickly learned that I couldn't be everything to everyone. We did not have the speed to make money in all areas of construction. I decided to specialize in flooring and kitchen cabinets. The flooring was perhaps the easiest way to make money: my only financial outlay was for labor; our customers supplied all materials. I would continue doing flooring until 2002, when my body told me it was time to stop. Initially, I bought the kitchen cabinets for installation, but it seemed our suppliers were always short one or two cabinets per kitchen, which always seemed to delay completion of jobs. So I decided I'd make my own cabinets and countertops. I purchased a few large tools and set up a small shop in my home at 31 Sycamore Drive in Burlington.

This didn't work too long because my neighbors started complaining to the township about my running a business at my home and the congestion we caused on the street. I had to go out and find a shop, which I did—in a rundown building on River Road in Riverside, New Jersey. The rent was right, and there was adequate parking. There were a few downsides to the space. It was broken up into small sections, which caused me to constantly be changing our setup, and the other tenants in the building seemed always to be complaining about the smell of our lacquer and contact adhesive. (I must say, the smell is breathtaking.)

Within six months, I had sixteen employees plus Ed VanSciver. A few months after I started Kruger Limited Corp., Ed was no longer working for the management company. If there was a person I truly trusted in business, it would be Ed VanSciver. We started working together taking only $100 per week. Honestly, I didn't even take the $100 per week until after three years. Ed couldn't afford to work for so little money, for he had just married Linda and had a new son, Brian, in addition to the other three boys from his first marriage.

Now is the time to mention that before Ed married Linda, he asked me to be his best man. I regret to this day that I refused. Ed was at least fifteen years older than Linda, and I truly didn't think the marriage would last. I couldn't have been more wrong. I now know that Linda gave unconditional love to Ed and gave him the life he truly deserved. Ed and Linda stayed married until Ed's death in September of 2003. Ed and Linda both asked me to be the godfather of their firstborn son, Brian, and I am proud to say I accepted. You will hear more of my godson Brian in this writing. Ed had no options other than getting a job as a salesperson selling to multifamily dwellings, and he was really good at it.

As I mentioned earlier, my profit margin didn't permit me to take pay. But I did buy tools, which increased productivity. The first few years were really lean. It's about this time that my opinion of workers changed. Previously, I'd assumed that if you treat people right, they would do a good job for you. I was wrong. They would do a good job for you only if you manage them. With sixteen people, I could not manage them all. I did not have core employees, so as people left, I did not replace them. By August of 1988, I was down to two employees.

CHAPTER 9

The Move to Shamong: a Long Way from Southwest Philly

Kitchen views then and now

IT WAS ABOUT THIS TIME that Mary got the urge to move. Her career at Lincoln Property was really taking off and, thank God, she was compensated well. She wanted to live by water: river, ocean, lake—it didn't matter. She found this very nice property on a small lake in Shamong Township, New Jersey, which I fell in love with immediately. It had enough property that I could build on without too many problems. It was basically in the woods and no one would complain about noise from my woodshop, so it was ideal. I could work at home again. Mary and I extended an offer and it was accepted. Closing would be December 30, 1988.

We immediately got our home in Burlington ready to sell. Ironically, when the real estate salesperson came to our home, she expressed concern that we only had one bathroom. When we were ready to move, I had to put a partial bathroom in after having lived there for thirteen years with one bathroom. Please keep in mind that we'd paid $36,000 for the house in Burlington. Mary decided, with the help of the Realtor, to list it for $160,000, and you guessed it, no one came. Our agreement of sale for the new property in Shamong gave us no contingencies, with December 30 coming around. Both Mary and I decided we'd better go get a swing loan (a loan for the down payment to carry us through until our Burlington home was sold). We didn't sell the Burlington home until September of 1989. It sold for $116,000. The Realtor really gave us a bum scoop. That meant we paid two mortgages from January through September, and that meant we couldn't afford to furnish our new home. As a matter of fact, the original bedroom set that Mary had bought when we first got married would not stand up to another move. Therefore, we bought a box spring, a frame, and cardboard drawers at Bradlees discount store. We had no furniture whatsoever in our great room. We would live this way for a few years.

When I said I fell in love with the house, I meant I fell in love with it. At closing, we told the former owners that we wouldn't change a thing. We changed everything. When you drove down the hundred-yard gravel driveway, you felt you were really in the woods, because you really were in the woods. The only manicured area was in the front of the house, on either side of the walkway. The other side of the driveway backed up to wetlands. Mary and I would soon find out that the mosquitoes came across the driveway with doggie bags in which to take munchies home. That first summer was really bad for mosquitoes.

The second summer we had four half-acre bug zappers that we turned on early in the season, before the mosquitoes became overwhelming. We knocked out most of the population before the season began. Speaking about the other side of the driveway, the former owner would just throw branches, leaves, and grass cuttings there. In the upcoming years, on that side of the driveway, I would build four pole barns and three utility buildings. I started taking down dead trees and trees that had fallen, and I cut them up for firewood. At this writing, my firewood pile is three feet high and three hundred feet long. In the twenty-five years Mary and I have lived here, we've had the fireplace going twice, and that was with artificial logs. I bought a commercial-grade wood chipper, and I've put it to good use. I maintain a 50' x 300' buffer area between my woodpile and the driveway.

I should mention that I promised myself that I would not manicure any more than had already been manicured. I broke my promise. I manicure the entire front of our house, including the other side of the driveway in the wetlands. I have created a park-like environment, and in spring and summer, the most beautiful ferns grow. During the first year we lived here, we lost power forty-eight times. This definitely motivated us to purchase a generator. The first generator would run our television, our refrigerator, maybe a little fan, and the coffee pot. I failed to mention our house was totally electric, with an oil burner. Not being an electrician, I had no idea how to get our heater working using our generator. Thank God all the outages, for the most part, were in the spring, summer, and fall. After living here six years, we purchased a whole-house generator with an automatic switch. The maximum time we are without electricity is five seconds. This generator is big enough to run our home, including my shop at home, where I worked for eleven years.

When we first looked at the house, we were really pleased and fell in love with the front of the house. That was nothing compared to the back of the house, where we have a 200-foot, give or take, beachfront on a small lake. The lake is man-made and was formerly a cranberry bog, and for the most part is no more than three feet deep, except where our dock is. Yes, I built a dock. I determined how long the dock would be by having a person with a rope walk out until the water was over his head; in this area, the lake's depth is about six and a half feet deep.

This dock has a very interesting story. Up to this point, Mary had never yelled at me in front of a stranger. But in this case, I started and just about completed the dock while she was on a business trip. When the limousine brought her home, she noticed our new dock from the highway. And you guessed it, she tore into me like nobody's business.

After building our addition for the shop, I noticed we had the right terrain for an upper pond, a stream, and a lower pond with a waterfall. The noise can actually put you to sleep. After building the waterworks, I decided to build a series of decks with a bridge over the stream. With a tree growing out of the bridge, it really looks

interesting. Since the back of the house has sun most of the day, whereas the front of the house has very little sun, I created flower beds there, which ultimately grew to stone flower beds primarily on the shore. In the spring, we have thousands of daffodils and tulips. The impact is overwhelming. When summer comes, Mary plants annuals. I guess it's the German in me, because I truly love flowers.

I've developed a habit of planting trees in memory of people who have departed. We've got a lot of new trees that we've planted. I then found a place where I could buy shrubbery at a real reasonable price. I would say that I'm planting, nowadays, about fifty new shrubs every year. Unfortunately, only half of them survive. I have no idea why the survival rate is the same no matter how much I pay for the shrubs.

We have azaleas, rhododendrons, mountain laurel, Pierce japonica, and on and on. It really is beautiful in the spring and summer. I failed to mention that Mary and I both have a black thumb. Our good friend Gabe does the planting.

Once I started working with stone, I purchased my own cement mixer, and I guess I went a little crazy. There are stone walls in the back, front, both sides—all over the property. Offhand, I would say we have a thousand feet of stone walls from eight inches high to five feet high. This reminds me of a time when I was building a wall and asked Mary about the height. She indicated it was too high, so I took a few courses of stone off. I asked her to give her opinion again, and she said it was too low, so I put a few courses back on. I then asked her opinion, and she said it was too high. I waited an hour, did nothing, and asked her again. She said it was just right, when I'd done nothing, basically. She has learned to love to break my balls.

We have so many flower beds now, I have to purchase thirty yards of mulch every year, which takes my Saturday crew two weeks to put down. After dealing with the shrubbery and the flower beds, I started looking at the house very hard. The yellow siding made it look like a banana, and because of the addition and not being able to purchase the yellow siding, I had to save the siding I took down from the garage side for the additional front of the house, and put dark brown wood siding on most of the back and side of the house. I definitely didn't like that. So after a lot of coaching and about five years, Mary and I picked out a cultured stone, because of the overwhelming look. I had to build pent roofs sporadically in several areas of the house, which really added to the charm of the stone. The cultured stone is really concrete that is made to look like stone. I didn't save any money doing this, but I did save a footing, which I didn't need to do with cultured stone, thereby saving a considerable number of our plantings.

I then looked at our brick deck, which Mary and I had both learned to dislike because of the pointing. We contracted a mason and had stone laid on the upper and lower decks. The last change to the exterior of the house was the sliding door in our kitchen. We had a window, so if you wanted to go out on the deck, you had to walk through our great room and negotiate a sliding screen door, which was always a pain to open and close. After several years of discussing with Mary about putting a sliding door in our kitchen to replace the window, one morning she said okay.

Immediately after she left for work, I called my brother Jackie and told him to pick up the sliding door on his way into work. By the time she got home, the door was in. With Mary, persistence works, and I let Mary believe the interior of the house is hers.

One of the first things I did was replace the kitchen cabinets. We would work on that when we had nothing else to do, which seemed to be never. One morning after being without the kitchen for three months, I decided to finish the kitchen before I did anything else. The first thing I did was install ceramic tile in the kitchen, mudroom, and bathroom. Once we got started, it didn't take very long. The next thing I did was replace every door in the house. There were eighteen doors. At the time of this writing, our house is in the beginning stages of converting to gas, as opposed to oil. I think it's a good move.

CHAPTER 10

Our Immediate Family

IN 1983, SERGE (PICTURED ON left) was really having problems getting around, and I knew his days were numbered. We would walk to the mailbox at the end of the corner and have to stop three or four times for him to get his breath. One night I told him it was all right if he wanted to leave us. The following morning, Mary and I found him dead. He lived with us for twelve years, and the only thing he ever did wrong was have gas problems. I mention this for a reason. Shortly after Serge's death, we decided to address an ear infection that Mr. Spock (right) had. It was a very bad move. Within two months he was diagnosed with cancer, and he just continually got weaker and weaker. When I'd come home from work, I would find him in the same position as I'd left him in the morning. I would pick him up and take him outside, as he would not mess in the house. By this time, he'd developed bedsores. It broke my heart. So one morning I gave him enough tranquilizers to kill a horse. When I came home, he was just groggy. You must understand, I loved this dog and I felt that he knew I would never do anything to hurt him. Mary and I said good-bye to him. I put a plastic bag over his nose and mouth. Within thirty seconds, he was dead. I could not see taking him somewhere, where someone else would put him to sleep. I'll never do that again to anything or anyone. I buried Mr. Spock right next to Serge. While digging the grave, I got too close to Serge's coffin, and you guessed it, there was gas. I think he was telling me he was still with us.

During the time I worked for Langhorne Properties, Incorporated, I found a stray kitten and I brought her home. Mary and I decided to keep her. We had never had a cat before and had no idea how to care for a cat. It was a little gray cat that looked like a Russian blue. We named it Slick, thinking it was a male. That night, we took her to the veterinarian and were told it was a female. We changed her name to Slickie. She never got any bigger than two or three pounds. When we brought her home from the veterinarian, we stopped and purchased a litter box and litter. Once we put these two together, like lightning, she was in that box. The following day, we purchased a flea collar. Within a few minutes

of putting it on her, Mary called me and said how funny it was that she was trying to get it off. She wasn't trying to get it off. It was stuck under her bottom jaw. I removed the collar and actually gave her mouth-to-mouth resuscitation. She never forgot it and loved me until she died nineteen years later.

In 1984 we purchased a Doberman pinscher puppy and named him Spock 2. He was liver-colored and the first thing we did was have his ears cropped and his tail docked. He grew to be one intimidating-looking dog, but that little cat was still queen of the house, and he feared her all his life. He would give her a wide berth whenever she walked by. I say this because she would jump up and bite him just to keep him in line. Whenever someone would come to our home, we would have to introduce that person to Spock 2. I recall one time when the electrical inspector came to our home in Shamong and ignored the dog. The dog didn't ignore him. He bit him in the butt, just a little bit, to show that he was boss. Spock 2 lived to be twelve years old, and he also died of cancer. I buried him right next to Mary's parking spot at our home in Shamong.

In 1990, while installing a kitchen in Delsea Village Apartments in Millville, New Jersey, a little stray kitten came wandering by all by itself. I asked if it belonged to anyone and no one claimed it, so I decided to take it home, and surprisingly, Mary easily agreed to keep it. We had no idea what to call her until my brother-in-law Bruce came over and mentioned how long her tail was. He named her LT (short for "Longtail"). LT and Slickie got along like they were sisters. The only complication now was that we had two cats and three dogs. The only place to feed the cats was on the countertops, because the dogs would eat their food. So Mary encouraged me to build portable stairs, so the cats would not have to jump as they got older. I also had to cut holes in three doors to give them access to their litter box. Even though the cats are gone at this writing, the holes are still in the doors. LT died in 2005, and we buried her in Pitts Memorial Park.

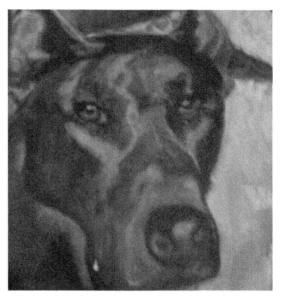

In 1996, we purchased another Doberman pinscher puppy and named him Spock 3. He was fawn-colored. Just like with Spock 2, we had his ears cropped and his tail docked. He also grew to be one intimidating-looking dog. He was truly Mary's dog. He loved her like no tomorrow and protected her like no tomorrow. He and Freddy (a dog I'd found in 1986) didn't get along well, and once at a jobsite, Freddy fractured Spock 3's leg, since Spock 3 was just a puppy. When we got him, our cat Slickie was older and also ruled over him. Spock 3 grew to be ninety pounds, and he was intimidated by a three-pound cat. She was the only thing that intimidated him. If I had to correct him, I would get two hits. I think if I tried three, he might've taken my hand. He lived to be nine years old, and I buried him right next to Spock 2, next to Mary's parking spot.

It was somewhere around 1995 that an old golden retriever kind of crashed our Fourth of July party. He was red in color, so naturally we called him Reds. Because he wouldn't go away, I put him in my garage and waited till our party was over. I let him outside, but he still would not go away, so we kept him. I am almost positive that he was half blind, because every time I gave him a treat, he would bite my hand, so I learned to throw treats. Spock 2 immediately proceeded to beat him up, and surprisingly, Freddy defended Reds, but as male dogs go, there has to be a top and a bottom, and Reds was at the bottom.

Reds lived with us for about two years. One morning while we were walking him—it was still dark—he disappeared. Mary and I were frantic because we had learned to love Reds as if we had known him since he was a puppy. We posted signs everywhere in our neighborhood, but most importantly at the general store about a mile away. The first person to contact us was one of our neighbors, who lived about a quarter mile away. She informed us that Reds had crashed one of her parties a few years before ours, and she'd kept him. Then one morning he disappeared on her as well.

Our second contact was from a Mrs. Wells, who told us that she had Reds. Mary and I immediately drove to her home, which was about six or seven miles away. It seems that Mrs. Wells was his original owner, and about four years earlier he had disappeared. When I did the math, I realized that Reds was now fifteen years old. Mrs. Wells said Reds looked so good and that if we wanted him, we could have him because she had congestive heart failure. It seemed when Reds was younger, Mrs. Wells told us, anytime there was a female dog in heat, Reds was gone for a few days. Mary and I were very happy to bring him back home. Reds would live with us for another four years. I buried him in our yard under a statue of Saint Francis along with many other different animals (friends). By my calculation, Reds lived to be nineteen years old. As a matter of fact, when ticks would bite Reds, they would fall off dead because of old age. Both of the leads came from the signs we posted at the general store. Something heart-touching that had to do with Reds was that once Mrs. Wells had given him to us, he would receive a Christmas card from her every Christmas. This went on for a few years, even after Reds died. The Christmas cards stopped. I assumed that Mrs. Wells had passed away.

One of the best things that happened in the first years of being in business was finding Freddy, in 1986. We were in Jersey City, converting apartments into condominiums for Gold Coast Realty, and the super on the job asked me if I wanted a dog. The dog was about a year old. He was a Belgian sheepdog, commonly referred to as a "long-haired shepherd." The super called him Harry. I immediately changed his name to Freddy to coincide with Freddy Krueger. It had a little more class. When I brought Freddy home for the first time, we were concerned that he might not get along with Spock 2, and honestly, it took him a little while, so he spent a few nights at our shop in Riverside. But finally Mary fell in love with Freddy as well, and he was permitted to come home to 31 Sycamore Drive. Freddy, Spock 2, and Slickie learned to live together quickly.

While Spock 2 and Slickie stayed home, Freddy would go to the shop and jobsites with me. Wherever I went, Freddy was there as well. He could mooch hamburgers at McDonald's or anywhere else we went. He could open the door to the truck if he had to go to the bathroom. He was smarter than a lot of the people I know. His only drawback was that he was afraid of thunder. Once at a property in Hazelton, Pennsylvania, during a thunderstorm he opened the door to the truck and entered a hallway in one of the apartment buildings. When I went to the truck for one reason or another, I discovered he was gone. Just about the time I went to the management office seeking help, maybe from the maintenance staff, to locate him, a tenant was on the phone reporting this big dog in her hallway. I was greatly relieved and learned to tie Freddy in the truck with just enough lead so he could go outside and go to the bathroom. Another time, when we were traveling on the turnpike at sixty miles an hour, Freddy opened the door and I had to grab him to prevent his jumping out to go to the bathroom. I then learned not to give that long of a lead while in the truck. Freddy was the kind of dog who never gave us any trouble whatsoever.

It was December 3, 1999, when Freddy became lethargic. I immediately took Freddy to our veterinarian, Tom Weiner. I think Tom knew what was wrong, but didn't want to tell me. He suggested that I leave Freddy there and stay and talk with him a little bit before I left, which I did. Three hours later, Tom called me and informed me that Freddy had passed away. Even after fourteen years, when I remember that Friday, I still cry. Next to Mary, Freddy was my best friend, and it broke my heart, and it broke Mary's heart when she came home and I had to tell her. I built him a coffin and wrapped him in a soft blanket and buried him in Pitts Memorial Park. He was the first one buried there.

On Monday, December 6, 1999, we called Tom Weiner and informed him that Reds had been having seizures both Saturday and Sunday, and they were continuous. He told us that even if he stopped having the seizures, he would never be right again. The only merciful thing to do was to put him to sleep. We asked Tom to come to our house. He did, and Mary and I kissed Reds good-bye and Tom gave the injections. I built him a coffin, and he was the second occupant of Pitts Memorial Park.

It gets worse still. The following Monday, December 10, 1999, Slickie died. We knew that it was only a matter time, because she had lost weight and really didn't look well. I calculated that we'd lost fifty-three years of combined friendship with our three friends: fifteen years, Freddy; nineteen years, both Reds and Slickie. This was for sure the worst ten days of my life. For you see, your relationship with your pets is exactly the same as with your family members.

After the deaths of Freddy, Reds, and Slickie, only Spock 3 and LT were still with us. Mary and I decided to go to a German shepherd rescue and adopt a German shepherd. We found one who was all black. It seemed she was found in Camden, just roaming the streets. By her looks, you could tell she was pedigreed. Mary thought she could be the replacement for Freddy. We named her Slickie,

but affectionately. Because she was afraid of everything, she became squirrely, so I named her Squirrelo. When I attempted to take her to the shop with me, she was so frightened that I decided she was better off being home with Mary and Spock 3, and that is where she would remain for the rest of her life. I really felt bad for her. She was afraid of everything. I mean everything under the sun: someone knocking at the door, noises you heard outside, when the heater went on, a ringing telephone, even the ceiling fan in the kitchen. She would live with us for six years, and in that time she started to develop seizures, which became increasingly worse until she had a seizure that lasted for hours, which ultimately killed her. She is buried near Mary's parking spot.

LT lived for two years after Freddy, Reds, and Slickie died. She is also buried in Pitts Memorial Park. The statue of Saint Francis is still standing guard.

After the death of Spock 3, it became quite apparent that Squirrelo was not a good dog for protection. So Mary and I again went to a German shepherd rescue, and that is where we met Stosh. He was nine months old, and we were told that he was a gift to his former owner from his former owner's girlfriend, and they'd had plans of getting married. They didn't get married and Stosh spent his first nine months in a cage. I never realized how much energy a nine-month-old puppy who'd been brought up in a cage had. He was game for anything: fighting, wrestling, and his favorite, tug-of-war, except he kept choking up on whatever the tug-of-war was for; sooner or later he would bite you, but never out of anger. He just wanted to win. As a matter of fact, at one time or another he bit everyone in our shop, including me more than once. I don't know where he picked up his job as being protector to me, Mary, our house, our vehicles, and our property, but he really takes his job seriously. (I truly wish half of the working people in the United States took their job as seriously.) I'm sure he would have no problem going after anyone who would hurt us.

When I am at the shop or outside and he loses eye contact with me, he gets extremely nervous and runs all around in a tizzy looking for me. He is by far the

best guard dog that we have ever had, in addition to being one of my best friends. At the time of this writing, he's getting older. He's just about ready to turn eight years old, and his back legs are not what they used to be. Frankly speaking, I have to help him get into the vehicle, and I pick him up so that he won't jump. I even have to help him get on the bed again. He is the most loyal friend I've ever had. He could be out traveling with me all day and not take a leak or dump anywhere, except on our property, at home, or at the shop. He is really good that way. The only problem we've ever had with Stosh was when we first got him. He was all the time bugging Squirrelo: he would nip at her and run. We even brought this to the attention of our veterinarian, and Tom told us that when she was tired of it, she would go after him. It took about four months, but she did go after him and he stopped bugging her. I failed to mention that he is also one of the most handsome dogs and gets compliments everywhere I take him. I'm absolutely sure, because of his intelligence, he could've been anything one could make a German shepherd. I'm also absolutely sure that if he precedes me in death, it's really going to break my heart.

To refer to this as merely a collection of dogs and cats does not give the feeling of what Mary and I have felt for these friends. I make sure that I thank God every day that I knew each and every one of those pets that have died. If Mary or I didn't mention their names every day, they would be lost and truly dead, and that would be a tragedy. They are as close as any family member could be. Mary and I had their pictures painted, and they are prominently displayed in our home.

It was sometime in 2010, after the death of Squirrelo, that Mary and I decided to again go back to the German shepherd rescue to look for a new friend. Since Stosh was with me all day, Mary was home alone. This is when we found Bella. At the time we got her, she was about two years old. At the time of this writing, she is now six years old. We got her on Valentine's Day, so we cannot forget her birthday. As we see it, she is a long-haired shepherd with probably twenty shades of brown in her coat. Honestly, most women would give their eyeteeth to have her coloring. She's the most affectionate dog we've ever had, always happy, never mean except to other dogs. That's merely the protection coming out in a German shepherd. She's downright silly, kisses everybody, and she loves to French kiss. I always tell people that she likes to French kiss and that she likes to lick her butt, and for the most part she doesn't bark—she howls. When she sleeps, she snores.

She really loves Mary, almost as much as she loves to eat. She has put on weight since we got her. I believe she weighed eighty pounds. She now weighs ninety-five pounds and eats diet food, she never runs—she kind of hops. She loves to make snow angels. It has to be her idea to go out. She's the only dog that Mary has allowed in her car, and when Mary takes her places, she sits like a human being with a chauffeur. Both Mary and I love her to death. She's just a happy dog that makes everyone around her happy. I wish a lot of people did the same thing. She really has brought a lot of joy to our home.

CHAPTER 11

Kruger Kitchens of Shamong, New Jersey

WHEN THE DAY CAME TO move our shop from Riverside to our new home in Shamong, it was a rainy day and I still had two employees. Since I was out bidding another job, they had to move the shop. But due to indifference or stupidity, they failed to cover our power tools with a tarp, and to make matters worse, they stopped for lunch in the pouring rain with no consideration for the tools in the back of the pickup truck. Naturally, when I found this out, I fired both of them. Now it was just me. I calculated a profit and loss statement and found out that if I paid everyone and everyone paid me, I would still owe $4,000. This was really disheartening. After being in business for three and a half years, I decided I'd work by myself without hiring anyone. Within a few months of working by myself, I discovered, after doing a new profit and loss statement, I was to the plus $1,000. This was very encouraging.

I continued to work by myself until September 1989. By that time, my nephew David Hansell had just graduated from high school and was willing to wash my two trucks on the weekend. He was working for a muffler shop at that time, and after talking with him, I discovered he was working for minimum wage. Shortly after learning this, I made him an offer to come work with me for more money. I guaranteed him he would work at least forty hours a week, maybe not in cabinetmaking or flooring, maybe cutting my grass. He accepted and has been with me since. At the time of this writing, he's been with me for twenty-four years. I've learned to love him like a son.

It was in October 1989 that I decided to expand my garage by another 400 square feet. My brother Jackie came down from Bristol and stayed a few days while we framed out the addition. I upgraded everything in our addition: windows, lighting, insulation, and most important, HVAC. My memory kept sliding back to the winter of 1988, when I first moved to Shamong, with no heat in our garage, other than when the clothes dryer was on. I was constantly putting the dryer on. It was a cold winter.

With this addition, I had a real spray room with an adequate exhaust. Prior to our construction, I would open the garage door and spray out into the parking lot, and place the cabinet-door spray boards all around the ground. When it rained, I was out of business.

After being in business for nearly five years, the vast majority of our sales had been with one managing agent, Community Realty Management (CRM). This kept me very concerned about having all my eggs in one basket. When employees of this company went to other companies, they asked me to come to their new jobsites, which meant I was growing.

My brother Jackie had been working at U.S. Steel for about twenty-five years in January 1990, when he called me and asked if I could use him in our business. He explained that the union had planned to strike, and it was going to be a long strike. When the union did strike, U.S. Steel decided to close Jackie's part of the company, and we've been working together since. Nowadays, he only works two days a week because he is sixty-nine years old at the time of this writing. Some people have problems with working with family. I don't, particularly not with Jackie. Probably because I have the utmost respect for his ability, opinion, and character. When we first started working together, I would spend a considerable amount of time explaining how to get the job done. Jackie would listen, and then do things his own way anyway. I gave up. He generally gets things done just as efficiently as I would. Today one of his major duties is to keep the machinery and small tools working. He has developed a relationship with the tool suppliers. It's a true joy having Jackie working with me.

With Jackie coming to work with me, he asked me about another person, Cyril Gordon, who was also a former employee at U.S. Steel. Cyril had worked kind of part-time with me at our Riverside location, but was not all that dependable. This made me real apprehensive about employing him, but Jackie assured me that Cyril would show up and do a good job. Jackie must have had some control over Cyril.

There were several other men/boys who worked with us in the early 1990s. One of them was Greg from Riverside, who worked nights as a guard at the state prison in Bordentown, New Jersey. With these four people, including me, we grossed over $400,000 in sales in 1991. This was by far the best year I'd had up to that point, and every year thereafter our volume increased. We grew to a point of over $2 million in sales in 2007. Gradually we added additional people at a slower pace. This gave me the opportunity to really spend time and develop people. Some of those people turned out to be the core people that are with me today.

Another one of those people is Brian Golden. In my entire life, I never saw anyone work as fast as Brian can, and with a great degree of accuracy. Brian proved to me that one man could put in a kitchen by himself. As a matter of fact, Brian has put two kitchens in by himself, and I failed to mention, in one day. Brian is still with me as of this writing.

Another person who came in 1993 was Jeffrey VanSciver. I mentioned earlier my good friend Ed VanSciver. He called me one day and asked me if I could give Jeffrey a job. I naturally said yes, because I'd always liked Jeffrey, remembering that he'd helped me at my former father-in-law's house and at his father's house when he was a lot younger. He was just coming back from Florida after having lived with his mother. Within a few hours, Ed was here with Jeffrey and all his personal belongings. I put him up at our home for a few nights and then found a place for him to live in Browns Mills, New Jersey, with one of my nephews, Steve Hansell. I lent him a car before he bought his own, and he's been with me ever since, except when he got married.

I'm not sure when or where, but I felt in my heart that God had told me that Jeffrey was going to be my responsibility for the rest of my life, and I really take that seriously. I encouraged him to find a tutor to help with his scholastic shortcomings, which he did, and I'm proud to say that it actually did work well. Jeffrey always had a good heart and was strong as a bull. He would lend someone his last dollar, which forced me to help him maintain his finances. He found a room with a family in Tabernacle, New Jersey. He lived with that family for a good number of years. He worked anytime you asked him. He would help other people and they would pay only a portion of his worth. He works really hard and has never cried or complained. I forced him to save money, and he was really doing well in that area. He didn't owe anyone anything. He owned two vehicles and had several thousand dollars in the bank. As a matter of fact, one of his vehicles was an antique 1969 Pontiac Firebird.

I guess at this time I should explain that I laid out three criteria for his personal love life. First, she had to be over fifteen. Second, she could not be mentally challenged. Third, she could not have children. That worked for a while because he did follow the rules until he met a woman who looked like a linebacker for the Philadelphia Eagles. I believe Jeffrey thought she really loved him. She came from a family that definitely had class, and the next thing I knew, they were getting married. To her credit, she really did clean Jeffrey up. He would shave and get haircuts. He really looked clean. I always told Jeffrey to practice safe sex: that is, not to catch any sexually transmitted diseases and not to create any children until you were married. That part, he didn't listen to. He assured Mary and me that she wasn't pregnant, after telling other family members of mine that she was. She lived in Havertown, Pennsylvania, which was not around the corner, but an hour to an hour and a half away. Consequently, when they got married, Jeffrey was going to move in with her at her parents' home, meaning that he had to quit his job working with us, which he did. I never felt that this marriage would work, and when I received an invite to the wedding and reception, I declined and sent a gift. And in my opinion, and in my opinion only, she wanted to get married to produce a child for her parents.

I understand that after Jeffrey got married and moved to her parents' house, Jeffrey got a job in a bagel shop and at a shop where countertops were made. He didn't last very long in the countertop place, but did at the bagel shop. Jeffrey always had somewhat of temper, and she really knew how to press his buttons. So after about six months of living at her parents' home, she provoked Jeffrey and he smashed a wall with his hand. She filed charges and Jeffrey was mandated by the courts to attend anger-management classes. He also had to leave her parents' home. So one day Jeffrey showed up and asked for his job back. He got his room back with the family in Tabernacle, but his problems had just started.

The first thing was that the money he had saved was gone. The '69 Pontiac had been towed to the junkyard because he was not allowed to park it in her parents' driveway, and it seemed he owed everyone. Making things even worse was the fact that the court imposed such a high child-support number. I take some of the credit for this because I allowed him to go to court with a female attorney who could only say, and I quote, "That is regulations." She didn't have an ounce of fight in her body. Some of this, I blame on the program. One of their sayings is "live and let live." By this time, I was a member of the program, so I allowed Jeffrey to handle his own money and be responsible for his own actions. This was not a good move. Within a few years, I realized just how much trouble Jeffrey was in. It was in March that I told Jeffrey I would be holding his checkbook so he could get out of his financial situation. I would be holding his checkbook because he was complaining about the bank service charges that had been charged to his account. The number was $281 in NSF charges year to date, and it was only February. Since then, Jeffrey has never paid any NSF charges.

Jeffrey and I wrote a budget for Jeffrey to follow. It didn't leave him with much walking-around money, or even money for his necessities. He had a bill that he'd incurred, sometime in the late 90s, with a credit card that he had applied for and received without my knowledge. I think he owed the credit card company, when it started, about $900, but the judgment from court totaled out to be somewhere around $3,200. The collection agency perfected a garnishment of his wages. He also claimed his son, Jeffrey, on his income taxes. His divorce papers plainly stated he couldn't, because he owed the IRS somewhere around $1,100. His cell phone was turned off, and Verizon claimed that he owed them $750. Of that $750, approximately $200 was due to early termination of his contract. So in essence, they were going to charge for terminating his contract early. We paid Verizon $550 and told them to scratch their ass for the rest. Ironically, Verizon never chased him. It took approximately three years for Jeffrey to be on sound footing financially. Frankly speaking, I have no idea how he survived those three years, from a financial standpoint.

As I said earlier, Jeffrey moved back in with that family in Tabernacle. But Mary was always concerned because they were elderly, and if they ever decided to move, Jeffrey would find himself in a pickle. Due to Mary's insistence, we went out and found a trailer in a relatively nice trailer park and purchased it for him. Though the trailer was a real piece of shit, we fixed up the interior, after several thousand dollars in material and labor. Ironically, Jeffrey really takes care of it. He has so much pride in ownership that when I get shrubbery for my home, Jeffrey gets some for his.

When I put up Christmas lights, Jeffrey puts up Christmas lights. And by the grace of God, maybe this spring or summer we will take care of the exterior of his home also.

Most of the people who know the relationship between Jeffrey and me think that I'm overly good to him. Let me straighten this out right now. Without Jeffrey, I would be in deep, deep shit. For you see, it's my thinking and Jeffrey's arms and strength. Also, he is willing to do whatever I ask him to do, no matter how cold or hot it is outside or uncomfortable in the places that I make him work. For example, in the dead of winter, I ask him to clean out the pump for our outside waterfall. I know how cold the water is, but he never complains. When it snows, we start at five or six o'clock in the morning. I am in the pickup truck plowing, and Jeffrey is with a snowblower, leaf blower, or shovel, addressing the places where it's impossible for the truck to do the job. Sometimes we work until well after dark and do my driveway, my two neighbors' driveways, my shop parking lot, and sometimes the auto mechanic's parking lot. In summation, I'm very grateful to have Jeffrey with me, and so is Mary.

It came to the point that we were so busy that I employed someone to work three nights a week in my garage/shop building countertops. This would go on for about eleven years until one Friday morning, the building inspector showed up at my house with an alleged complaint about my doing commercial work out of my garage, and for the four illegal pole barns. The pole barns housed my antique vehicles. This was devastating to me at that time because I now had to find a new place to work, which would never be as convenient as working at home. For you see, I could get up in the morning, put coffee on, go out to the shop, and spray cabinets before I'd had my breakfast, showered, and gotten ready for work. This now was a thing of the past. I also paid no rent at home. Now I would be paying rent or something.

I immediately started looking for a building for rent, where I could move my shop. I'd looked at several buildings—and I could've made several of them work, but I would be sacrificing efficiency one way or another—when I remembered where I'd had a fiberglass hood made for one of my cars. I observed that a lot of room was not being used, because the owner was downsizing and probably was looking to retire.

Since I always believed in "nothing ventured, nothing gained," I decided to talk to the owner of the building about renting some space. This building was right around the corner from my house—no more than a mile away—which meant, actually, I could walk to work if necessary. To my surprise, he agreed to rent me 1,000 square feet for $500 a month, with the understanding I would have to supply my own heat and air, and use a common bathroom, along with fitting up my space, which meant I had to build some walls and doorways. This also allowed me to set up my shop the most efficient way possible.

It took me two months of Saturdays, and maybe days during the week when we were slow, to build out our space. So in February of the year 2000, we moved into our new location at 148 Stokes Road in Shamong. Probably the best move I've made in a long time. One drawback to this setup was that Fred Van Pelt, the owner of the building, also ran his business with one other employee out of the same location. Fred's business was fiberglass, and he made some really unique things.

By this time I had eight employees, and frankly, they were really good. I say this because at home I worked from seven in the morning till six at night five days a week, and Saturdays from eight to one. I very soon learned that with the additional space—the 1,000 square feet that I rented from Fred plus the areas in other parts of the building that Fred allowed me to use for storage—the number of hours of work was decreasing, ultimately bringing it to a quit time of 3:30. No more overtime and no more comp time.

This had worked great for about two years when Fred came to me and asked if I were interested in purchasing the building, because he wanted to retire. I had a big decision to make, because Fred wanted a big number for the building. I asked him if I could continue to pay him rent and save money to purchase the building for cash, and within five years, I did purchase the building for cash. The remainder of the building had to be fitted to accommodate a cabinetmaking business. This was not cheap. I had to knock down walls and the second floor. We installed new heating, new garage doors, wall coverings of metal; built additional walls; dropped the ceiling; and installed air-conditioning. We purchased and installed a state-of-the-art, explosion-proof spray booth. I find it interesting that when we were about ready to put in a new heater, our plumber suggested we install radiant heat. What a great idea this was, because when we open the garage doors, the cold air comes in and warms up very quickly. After the lines were laid on the floor, we poured four inches of concrete to create a nice flat surface.

With the new shop, I had the opportunity to purchase machinery that would make our operation even more efficient. Most notable was a forklift. I now could buy plywood in large quantities, which saved us considerable dollars. Instead of using two guys to unload a truck of plywood, we now could do it with one, and plywood could be stacked as high as sixteen feet. We started using pallet jacks, rolling tables, and wood carts. We bought a blade-sharpening system, which required about forty square feet. Using the forklift, we built overhead storage to store the system. All our additional labor-reducing measures meant that we could hold the line on price increases, ensuring us additional sales.

Part of the crew that worked at my home making countertops was big Danny. He had a son, Matt, who was fourteen, who started working with us on Saturdays. When Matt graduated from high school, he started working with us full time. Matt is now thirty-five, and he is still with me.

Last but not least was Brian VanSciver, Jeffrey's brother and my third godson. I think he started in '96 or '97 as a fifteen-year-old. When Brian worked Saturdays and attended high school during the week, Jeff would pick him up and take him home. He took shop and worked half-time with us and half-time at school. When he graduated, he said he was going to go to college, and he actually did enroll. I think he went two semesters part-time while working full time with us. Even with my encouraging him to return to college, he never went back. That was totally his choice, not mine. I still believe that once young people have money in their pocket, college doesn't have a snowball's chance in hell, as a rule. Brian has become a great joy to work with. He is, honestly, a diamond in the rough. First, he has the intelligence, and second, the social skills to talk with customers and fellow employees alike. As a matter of fact, in 2009 Brian became, and still is, the shop foreman, the most important job in our business. He readily takes on this responsibility. If I'd had sons, I would've hoped that one of them turned out just like Brian. He has my respect and admiration, and at his age, the sky is the limit. Honestly, he runs the business.

I think it was in 1998 that I found one of the best employees I've ever worked with in my life, and I mean in my life, and that is Herb. I hired him on a fluke. Just goes to prove that the best-laid plans of men are not always right; many good things happen due to luck or accidents. The fellow who was doing our grass cutting, and who still is, had an extra man and asked if I could use him. I have always felt that if I could do a person a favor, I would. I really didn't interview Herb, or anything else. It was my brother Jackie who brought it to my attention just how good this guy actually was. Herb would watch you do something, and if you went to the bathroom and came back, he was doing what you were doing. Within fifteen or twenty minutes, he would tell you how to do it faster and better.

Herb was about nineteen or twenty when he first came to work with us. I would later find out that he was also an excellent mechanic, welder, and soon to be a great auto-body person. He is also a pleasure to work with, never has an attitude or complains—a real humble, stand-up guy. If I'd had a second son, I would have liked him to be exactly like Herb. I was honored when Herb asked me to be godfather to his son Brandon, my fifth godson, and equally honored when Herb and his wife, Connie, asked Mary and me to be godparents to their daughter Yztel, my fourth goddaughter. Herb still works with me at my house on Saturdays, for four hours, and at the time of this writing, my godson Brandon, who now is eight years old, comes with him as a rule. The rule is if he does well in school, he can come; if not, he cannot. His mom is very serious about school.

It was somewhere around 2002 that we stopped doing floors. The only reason we stopped was that I noticed my knees were starting to give out. I've always said I'd never ask someone else to do something I was not willing to do as well. My body was telling me it was time to stop. Also, we had enough cabinetmaking business to keep us more than busy. This went well until 2008, when the bottom fell out of the economy. To that point, we had been doing primarily multifamily dwellings. When we were doing apartment buildings, it wasn't required that we go and sell every job. Most of the time, our customers would call us from whatever property they were at and actually give us measurements. If we hadn't expanded into more residential kitchens, I'm not sure that we would have survived as a business. Also, it was very good for the crew because now they were forced to hone their skills, which I view as a positive, and getting right to the point, they got really damn good.

Prior to 2008, virtually all our kitchens were built of natural (no stain) red oak, with a five-piece flat-panel door. Since 2008, we have really diversified. We now work with several different species of wood, including cherry, maple, walnut, and poplar, with natural and stained finishes, including colored lacquers. Our kitchens now are totally customized. I mean to say, we really build some weird stuff now, but that's what our customers want, and their goal is our goal. Of course, the price of kitchens has increased considerably. We even had to go to another price guide, which is much more complicated than what we were accustomed to. Today, we may be able to finish three custom kitchens in two days, whereas before, we could do nine or ten multifamily-dwelling kitchens in two days.

In addition to the poor economy, one of the customers with whom we were doing $750,000 a year decided to sell his entire portfolio. When we met the new owners, they required that we be responsible for 100 percent of all construction and repairs to their properties, which included roofing, siding, plumbing, windows, drywall, and so on. If we committed to the new owners to complete their requirements, we would've had to pass on all our existing customers, and we would have had all our eggs in one basket. I had promised myself that I would never put myself in that position again, remembering how I had felt when CRM was my one and only customer, or close to it. I had no option, in my opinion, but to give up that $750,000 a year. That would have been over 33 percent of our annual business in 2007. During this period and in other periods of slow sales or economy, I've never laid someone off, unless they were hired as temporaries.

Prior to our move to our new shop at 148 Stokes Road, I was working on Saturdays. I guess I could never get out of that habit of working on Saturdays (due to my retail experience), so I would bring in a crew of younger people in the beginning. We would work at my shop in my home, getting a head start on the work of the following week. The crew included my godson Brian VanSciver, Matt Lewis, Brian Golden, and my nephew Jimmy. The year was 1997. I mention this for one reason, because all four of these men are still with me today.

In March 1993 I hired my nephew Jimmy, Walter and Phyllis's son. He worked with us for a few years and then resigned. Jimmy was young and hadn't been exposed to the workforce. I believe he just got bored. My health started getting bad in 2001, and by 2008 it was worse. It was real bad, and frankly, I needed a replacement for myself, just in case. Jimmy and I spoke, and he came back to work with us and took on the residential end and has done a fine job. He's really brought some challenges to our workforce. I view David, Jimmy, and Brian as my replacement. I'm sure it will work.

CHAPTER 12

My Cars

ONE OF OUR WEDDING GIFTS from Mary's Aunt Anna was a 1956 four-door sedan, 265 V-8 Chevrolet Bel Air. It was fourteen years old when we got it, and we still have it today. Though it's not driven very often, when we first got it, it wouldn't go over forty miles an hour. I think I know why: Aunt Anna was the only person I've ever known in my life who received a ticket for going too slow in a 25-mile-an-hour zone in Bayonne. Mary drove this car for the first years of our marriage. At this writing, we've been through interior changes, motor and transmission rebuilds, and probably most important, paint jobs—plural. It is currently candy-apple green and pearl white, with white and green rolled and pleated interior.

The next car I bought—from my brother Stanley, at Mary's insistence—was a 1974 Corvette Stingray. Ironically, Mary has only driven the vehicle three times, and we've had it since 1989. The car has always looked great. When I first got it, it was some weird gray, basically a no-go showboat. If you turned the windshield wipers on, the only way they would work is if you opened the door. Turn signals worked, I think, by pushing in the cigarette lighter. The number of wiring harnesses that have been replaced in this vehicle is ridiculous. All the electrical problems came from someone changing the front and rear to a 1980. Please consider that Corvettes are fiberglass and have a real severe grounding problem. Currently it's painted pearl white, much better looking than that gray.

My third car was a custom 1954 Ford six-cylinder. This car has a story behind it. When I was younger, my brother Walter had a '52 Ford. The 1952, 1953, and 1954 Fords all kind of looked alike. If I have not mentioned earlier, I'll make it clear now: My brother Walter could drive. He would get the most out of any engine, even though he was beating the hell out of it. The year was 1994 and Walter had just passed away, and I wanted to build something, I guess as a tribute to Walter. While driving to Atlantic City one day, I noticed this old Ford sitting in a semi-junkyard. I inquired at the office and was told that it was available for $300. It didn't run, the interior was a mess, and it was full of rust—big-time rust. That did not dissuade me.

When I was presented the title, I noticed the former owner was Joe Varano, the same name as one of the guys from Red Cedar Hill. I made inquiries and was delighted to find out that my buddy Joe was the father of the fellow selling the vehicle. In addition, I found out the Joe and his wife, Maureen, lived only a few miles from Mary and me. I was reacquainted with Joe after about twenty years. The Lord moves in mysterious ways.

Now that I had this car, I needed someone to work on it. Into my life came one of the people who would go on to become one of my very best friends, Michael Kloss. Mike was a brother to Donna Kloss, who worked with me for a short period at Shoe Stop stores in Hammonton. I was not aware that Michael was a mechanic for one of the local repair shops, and he did extra work at night and on the weekend. My intention was to build one fast rocket and we did. First, we had to find a new engine. Unfortunately, all newer engines were 12-volt electrical systems, whereas the '54 Ford was a 6-volt system. That meant all the wiring in the vehicle had to be changed. Second, the engine compartment had been modified to accept a new engine and transmission. The three-quarter cam engine came out of a Mustang, and the transmission was a combination of a C4 and C6 Ford transmission. The vehicle had to be sandblasted to ensure we got all the rust—there was a lot of rust—and we painted it flip-flop white. It was one striking-looking vehicle. The interior I had rolled and pleated in red and white, with racing seats. Since I only live about five miles from Atco Raceway, Michael and I took it down to see how fast it would go. After about six months of working on the vehicle, I was pleased to see it do mid-12s (seconds) in a quarter mile. In the past twenty years, I've repainted the vehicle twice. Currently it is "chameleon" (it changes color as you walk by, literally).

As I said earlier, Michael and I became real good friends. In 1994, unknown to me, I started to have a problem with alcohol. Michael already had a problem with alcohol, and I spent many summer Sunday afternoons drinking with Michael while working on the Ford. I think it was in 1995 that Michael and Kim moved to

South Carolina. Shortly thereafter, Mike informed me that Kim was pregnant and asked me to be the godparent to Samantha, my second goddaughter and my fifth godchild. When Michael and Kim got married, I was honored when Mike asked me to be his best man. I wish two things: that I would have been around more when Samantha was growing up, and that Mike and Kim lived closer.

In 1998, my brother Donny had been dead for two years. He had left his 1988 Monte Carlo SS to our niece Lisa, my sister Sophia's daughter. The car was parked behind my sister's house for two years, and since I knew that Donny loved that car, I made an offer to Lisa to purchase the car and she accepted. So, my nephew David and I got a new battery, a little gas, and some starting fluid, and fired that bugger up and drove it onto our trailer. It really is nice-looking and sounds like a million bucks. It just doesn't move.

In 2001, I purchased something that I'd always wanted: a 1970 Porsche 911 Targa, black on black. This is the most show-quality car I have, and God, is it quick. It has the strongest second gear I've ever seen. Its only drawback is that the brakes suck. Once on a back road, I was doing about 130 mph when I had to hit the brakes. I stood on the brake with both feet, and it seemed to take forever to stop. From then on, I decided that before I'd get on it again, I'd make sure nothing was coming and that I had adequate room for stopping. Another thing I learned about this car was the cost of repairs. It has two three-barrel carburetors. They had to be rebuilt, which required me to ship them to Arizona for the rebuild, at $800 per carburetor.

In the spring of 2013, I purchased a 1983 El Camino Super Sport. To say it was rough is an understatement. We spent two weeks on bodywork alone before we painted it metallic black with red pin-stripes and red lettering. I had the carpet removed from the interior and had the floor and truck bed sprayed with Rhino Linings liner (used in place of a bed liner). The purpose of eliminating the carpet inside was that Stosh travels with me a lot and sheds too much hair. I can simply open the doors, get a leaf blower, and blow the hair out of the vehicle. I purchased new bumpers, had seats reupholstered, changed the interior door panels, replaced the headliner, re-covered the dashboard, and painted the entire interior black, including the hanging carpet. I still have a problem with leaking oil, and I am forced to park it on gravel. It also is a no-go showboat.

It would be a sin if I didn't mention my 1984 Dodge Ram 3/4-ton pickup truck. I purchased it from a multifamily property for $2,500 well over twenty years ago. It included a snowplow. When I first purchased the truck, I purchased a cap for the bed and used it in our business. It was really one uncomfortable vehicle to drive in, and it killed your kidneys. When I could afford to have another vehicle, I retired the '84 Dodge pickup, affectionately called "the Tank" because it is a tank. I now use it for getting stone, dirt, mulch, and sometimes to remove stumps, but its primary purpose is to push snow at my home and at the shop. I have someone who comes to my home to repair the plow, and I have it checked every year. This, by the way, is the same guy who takes care of that old snowblower and other outdoor machines I have. He also is invaluable.

I bring up the Tank because this was our test vehicle. When I say test, I mean bodywork. I think we made every mistake you could possibly make. But thank God it was on the Tank that we first used the sandblaster, as we warped the hood. We didn't properly seal the bodywork, which caused the rust to come back. We replaced the entire truck bed at one point because the sides were ready to fall off. We had to replace the interior floor, because if you sat in the seats inside the cab, you could see the ground under your feet. Lots of rust, but it's quite dependable and I've registered it as an antique, which negates the inspections and yearly reregistering, which saves a lot of money. If anything were to go wrong with the Tank, I would repair it rather than replace it.

In the fall of 2014, I purchased a 1971 Volkswagen Beetle with decals of Herbie the Love Bug. *Herbie the Love Bug* was a film about a 1968 Volkswagen Beetle with a mind of its own and that mindset was racing. As of March 2015, I haven't started restoring this vehicle. My intentions were to eliminate the Herbie the Love Bug decals, but the majority of my friends that have seen this vehicle think I should keep them, so I will.

All of the vehicles mentioned are between twenty-six and sixty years old, making them qualify as antiques. I have eight: five of them are parked in the pole barns that I've built; the other three sit outside. The only vehicle I drive on a regular basis is the '83 El Camino. I never take them to car shows, or anything of that nature. I pull them all out on the Fourth of July. That is the only time they get displayed.

Talking of the Fourth of July, prior to my mother's death in 1985, my brother Stanley would have a yearly gathering at his home to celebrate one of the three holidays of summer. My brother Stanley gave this party for several years. So in the summer of 1989, Mary and I decided to have our families over on the Fourth of July. In the beginning, it was just my brothers and sisters, and Mary's sister and brother-in-law, Bruce. It then grew to nieces, nephews, business associates, and friends. It grew to between 250 and 300 people every year. Mary and I like to see our family and friends at something other than a funeral. After the first few years, it became apparent that Mary and I were not equipped to cook for that many people, so for the last twenty-one years it has been catered by someone who has become our good friend, Louie. In the beginning he brought his three young sons, who helped their dad. His sons have grown up to be fine young men. His oldest son, Frankie, recently became a father, and his middle son, Vinny, got married in the fall of 2014. The youngest son, Anthony, is still in college. Louie has always been able to acquire a lifeguard for us. We've seen young people start and finish college, as they started as our lifeguard before going to college and finished when college was over. We also hired a DJ, and that same fellow, Bob McGuire, has been the DJ for the last twenty years.

In the beginning I either attempted to borrow a tent or rent one, but I found it much more convenient to buy our own. Our guests know that our party starts at two and ends at six, and it's always on the Fourth of July. That's one day I don't think the government will move to a Monday. No invitation is needed. When someone's invited, they're invited for life. Surprisingly, with that many people, everyone behaves. I'm still amazed at that. Jackie and Donny had always maintained a relationship with the Pitts side of our family, so when it came to the Fourth of July, I started to invite some of the Pitts relatives. It still bothers me that I never

made any attempt to develop a relationship with them prior to then, because unlike my father, they're really fine people.

My first invites were to my cousin Jimmy and his wife, Helen, and my cousin Philip. His wife Snook had passed away sometime in the early- to mid-1980s. Jimmy and Philip both had the last name of Pitts, and they were the sons of my Aunt Beulah, who was my father's sister and who still lived in Bowling Green, Virginia. I was very pleased to see her attend at least one of my Fourth of July parties before her death. I mention Bowling Green because Aunt Beulah's children—Philip, Jimmy, Ed (also known as "June Bug"), Warren, Oakey, Hoppe, June, and Patty—also lived close to her.

I also got to know my Aunt Joan, who also was my father's sister. I was honored and privileged to have gotten to know my Aunt Joan and her husband, Ed Thompson. These people were definitely the salt of the earth, with all the class and humility that I strive to obtain. Uncle Ed passed away in 1995 and Aunt Joan passed away in 2006. I really got to know Aunt Joan well. She even took me to a family reunion on Long Beach Island, New Jersey, with the family of my aunt Mary Pitts Sprague, whom I never met because she  passed away years ago. Joan and Ed are really missed on the Fourth of July and throughout the year. They had four girls and four boys. Their names are Linda, Terry, Ronnie, Bobby, Jeannie, Norann, John, and Billy. Please keep in mind that their children are my age, and by the grace of God, we will continue to have this party for the rest of our lives.

CHAPTER 13

Reflections

ON MAY 7, 1990, WHEN I came home after installing a kitchen, Mary informed me that Sidra had called and told Mary that her father Jack (pictured right) had died. It had been a few years since I last spoke with Jack. I was not even aware that he was sick. This news really broke my heart, for there were four men in my life who definitely influenced the outcome of my character. The first was my brother Walter, second was Bert Actman, third was Jack Newberg, fourth and not least was Marvin Kaplan.

Jack was born in Brooklyn, New York, on February 6, 1919. That made him seventy-one years old, not old for 1990. I never did find out just what caused his death. Following Jewish custom, Jack was interred within twenty-four hours of death. I did attend his memorial service, and surprisingly, I was invited back to his home to celebrate his life with his family and friends. Naturally, Sidra and Stacy were there, and they were very pleasant with me, like all of Jack's family. Keep in mind, I was then forty-four years old and had come to the conclusion that Mary and I would not have children. It made me think that I really wanted a child, and I wanted to believe in my heart that Stacy was mine. This was the beginning of having a relationship with Stacy for the next several years, with each year that relationship growing stronger.

In early 1996 Stacy told me that her boyfriend, Jimmy, had asked her to marry him. This created a dilemma for me, for my belief was always that if two people live together prior to marriage, their wedding should be at their cost, not their parents'. But knowing that neither Stacy nor Jimmy had anything saved, I volunteered to pay for half their wedding and to advance them any funds that were needed, with the understanding that I would be paid back half. This seemed to sit well with both Stacy and Jimmy. Over the course of the next year and a half, I advanced them quite a bit.

Frankly, as hard as I tried, I still wasn't totally convinced that Stacy was my daughter. There were two situations that drove me closer to that belief. The first was when Shirley died in 1996, and the behavior of both Stacy and Sidra was downright shocking. I honestly don't remember any services for Shirley, except a gathering at Shirley's home for one reason or another. Because they were arguing, Stacy did not want her mother there and never mentioned it to her. I believe that kind of behavior is ruthless. I was also in disbelief at the way that both Sidra and Stacy went through Shirley's house claiming things. It is said that death and wills bring out the worst in people. This was living proof. A good example would be that Sidra asked me to bring a desk that she liked, and thought her brother Brian should have, to my house so Stacy could not lay claim to it.

From that time on, I became suspicious of everything either one said. It ended with Sidra claiming to me that it was necessary for me to rent my tuxedo at the same shop where the other members of the wedding party were renting their tuxedos. First of all, the shop was quite a ways from my home, and second, and more importantly, the driveway was very steep. When I drove my '74 Corvette up that driveway, it damaged my front end. I was really angry about that, and made it clear to Sidra. One thing led to another, and I was uninvited to the wedding, which took place on October 1, 1997. In all fairness to Stacy and Sidra, I would be the first to say that due to my drinking, I was a loose cannon. I did not speak to either one for quite some time. After about five years, I received a call from Stacy, in which she suggested we might get together.

We met for lunch at Mama Ventura's Italian restaurant in Marlton. There I met her daughter, Isabella, who was about six to eight months old. What a cute little baby. I learned that her and Jimmy's marriage lasted about six months, and she had then married a fellow by the name of Dylan. She appeared to be very happy, and there was no conversation about her mother at all. I was not going to be bold enough to ask for her phone number. I never heard from her again. At this writing, it's been twelve years since I spoke with her. I hope she has found peace in her life.

It was somewhere around 2006 or 2007 that I received a call from Sidra in the middle of the night, claiming that she'd broken down close to my home and was looking for help. This was the first time I can remember refusing to help someone when I could, but I did refuse. The last time I spoke with Sidra was in late 2013, when this writing was well underway. I think my ego might've gotten the best of me, because I wanted to tell her that I hadn't written anything terrible about her. I believed I could make her understand. Not five minutes into our conversation, she was asking me to subsidize her financially. Naturally, I said no. I thought we hung up rather cordially, and I was surprised that she called me back in about fifteen minutes and said that if there was anything in the book that she didn't like, she would be speaking to Mary and not in a positive nature. I simply said to her that maybe it wasn't a good idea that I'd called her. Hopefully, I will never speak with her again.

* * *

It was in the late autumn of 1992 when I found out that my brother Walter had terminal cancer. In a way, I couldn't believe it. I thought he was invincible and would live forever, or at least a lot longer than he was diagnosed to live. I'm absolutely sure that Walter was the number one influence on my life. Without him, no one else would've had the opportunity to impact our lives—I'm talking Jackie, Donny, and me—because he was the path out of the projects and on to bigger and better things. I know there is no way I can ever repay the sacrifices he made for me. I will be eternally in his debt in this life and in the afterlife. He was only fifty-six years old. You see, he was born May 17, 1936, and died on April 23, 1993. Hopefully, he would be joining his first wife Pat, for Pat had died October 1, 1978. She was born July 1, 1944. She lived to be thirty-four years old and died at her kitchen table at 42 Rolling Lane in Levittown of a massive heart attack, leaving behind their two sons, John and Walter.

My brother Walter always had good luck finding women, because he found Phyllis. A few years after Pat's death, when they got married, Phyllis brought her son Jimmy (who works with me now) and her daughter Lori into our family. Walter and Phyllis had two children, Philip and Matthew. I was honored when Walter and Phyllis asked me to be the godfather of Philip. As I got older, I know I gained Walter's respect, because in his mind my opinion counted, and he never let me forget it. As a matter of fact, we worked on a few jobs together, and he had no problem taking direction from me. This was a real ego booster for me. After Walter married Phyllis, Mary and I were invited every Thanksgiving, and that tradition continued on well after Walter's death. Knowing Walter was not an angel, I made it a point to tell him to make his peace with God, which I believe he did, and since he wasn't confined to a bed, I suggested he make his own final arrangements to make it easier on Phyllis. Walter died in April 1993, somewhere close around Easter, because in my heart of hearts I so much wanted him to resurrect on Easter Sunday. God I miss him and his humor, and I now say this prayer for him: "May the Lord bless and keep you. May the Lord make his face to shine upon you and be gracious unto you. May the Lord lift up his countenance upon you and give you peace." I say good morning to Walter and Pat every morning.

* * *

In November 1994, my brother-in-law Jack Kaufman passed away. Jack was born August 31, 1933. He was sixty-one years old. Jack was the husband of my sister Bobbie; to call her "Roberta," she might punch you in the mouth. They had two sons, John and Bill. Jack and Bobby were married somewhere around 1958. They lived a short time in an apartment in Ardmore, Pennsylvania. They ultimately bought a home in Morton, Pennsylvania, where they lived for the remainder of the thirty-six years they were married. Jack was a talented guy who had skills in many different areas. He became the go-to guy for my sister Sophia when she had problems. Jack was one friendly fellow who made everyone feel comfortable around him. He always had a big smile for everyone. Sometimes, I wonder why the good die young! After what to me seemed like a long time, my sister joined a ballroom-dancing group, and

I believe she has found peace in her life. But I know Jack is still number one in her heart and on her mind. That kind of old-fashioned love is what's missing in our society today.

* * *

In January 1996 my favorite brother, Donny, died. He was born February 28, 1950. He was just shy of forty-six years old, entirely too young to die. He died of that horrible, horrible disease known as AIDS. And yes, he was gay. As I stated

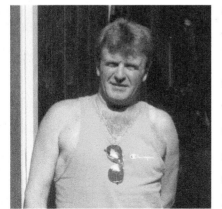

earlier in my writing, if someone had a problem with that, it was their problem.

I'm going to take this opportunity to mention some of the hypocrites in my family. They were very quick to condemn and shun Donny until homosexuality existed in their extended families. Frankly, it's not a big deal, but it certainly was when Donny was alive. I loved Donny and always encouraged him to practice safe sex. He didn't listen. When it was apparent something was wrong with him, I implored him to be tested. He did and he tested positive. He lived for about a year after his being tested. Knowing that I would not have an opportunity to spend any time with him, my sister Sophia, Donny, and I went on vacation to California. We started in La Jolla, went to L.A. and then to San Francisco. My sister Sophia had her own room, and Donny and I shared a room. In 1995 it was not known absolutely what caused AIDS. I'm ashamed to say that I wanted to take a shower before he did, being frightened of catching that horrible disease. When we returned home, I wanted to be tested, I was that terrified. But Mary assured me that I had nothing to worry about.

Toward the end, Donny was drinking and spending a lot of time in Atlantic City gambling; his credit cards were to the max. He always told me that he wanted to screw the credit card companies, and he managed to get them for about $60,000 at the time of his death. He also liked jewelry, really good jewelry. At times, he tried to give me certain pieces of jewelry, but I always declined because I didn't wear jewelry. After his death, I was informed that he had willed his house to me, which I in turn donated to AIDS research. My brother Donny and I had made an agreement several years earlier that if either one of us became terminal with zero quality of life, the other would help him to the other side. Again, I just did not have the courage to complete my end of the agreement. I'm sure Donny forgave me.

* * *

Halloween at National Institute of Health

On October 1, 1999, my great-niece died. Her name was Gia. What was truly sad was that Gia was born November 11, 1980, and her death was just shy of her nineteenth birthday. She had been born with a multitude of different ailments. The fact that she had any sort of life was due to my brother Stanley, who was her grandfather. Her father was my nephew Stevie, Stanley and Marge's youngest son. Stevie got married while in the military, and it appeared that his ex-wife was afflicted with some illnesses, which were passed on to Gia. Stan and Marge also had two sons, Michael and Chris, and a daughter, Andrea.

Chris was my first nephew to die. He was born on June 14, 1958. He died on January 23, 2012, at the age of fifty-three. Chris was his own man, which I

have always interpreted as a sign of strength. He started his own towing business without the help of anyone and did very well at it. Chris had one son, Joey, who inherited the business. At the time of this writing, Joey is trying to make a go of it. In my heart, I think he's going to be successful. He has the same drive his father had.

* * *

It was on Friday, March 16, 2007, at about five o'clock when Michael Hosgood, my great-nephew (Michael works with me), called and informed me that my brother Bill had been rushed to the hospital. A few hours later, Michael called back and told me that my brother Bill had passed away from a massive heart attack at the age of seventy-five. Bill was born on July 11, 1931. I was told that Bill's wife, Elaine, had just made a sandwich for him and then discovered him unconscious.

Other than the short time that Bill lived at 42 Rolling Lane with Walter, Stan, Jackie, Donny, and me in the slave/master living arrangement, and the time he helped me when Mary and I lived on Spring Lane in Levittown, for one reason or another, we had not known one another as men until I bought the building at 148 Stokes in which to operate Kruger Kitchens. Bill happened to come by when we were fitting up the building and, like all my brothers, just jumped in to give a hand. I know he had a good time doing it because he had been retired and babysat his great-granddaughter. I know he liked getting back into the thick of work. I've always believed that if I'm making money and someone is helping me do something, I should pay them. I say that because I offered Bill to work with Jackie and me for two days a week, which he gladly accepted. I'm really pleased I did that, because he got to know Jackie and me as men.

I recall that when I had been sober just about a year, Bill asked me if we could build and install a kitchen for his daughter, my favorite niece, Reneé. Building the kitchen was not a problem. It was to be installed in West Virginia. I bring this up for one reason. Bill, Jeffrey, and another fellow who works with me, Gabriel, and I left on a Friday night so we could install the kitchen the following day. We were going to stay overnight Friday and Saturday and come home Sunday. Knowing I would not be home for Mass on Sunday, I planned to attend a Saturday evening Mass in West Virginia. There are not a lot of Catholics in West Virginia. As a matter of fact, the closest church was about twenty miles away. I drove by myself in our truck. During Mass, the priest encouraged everyone not only to receive the body of Christ, but to drink the blood of Christ, commonly known as wine. Again, I'd only been sober for about a year. I looked up to God and said under my breath, "God, I know you're screwing with me." I did not receive the blood of Christ.

Gratitude and dependability were two of the things that most describe my brother Bill. I said earlier, other than my favorite niece Reneé, Bill had two other children: Reneé's older brother, Billy, and her younger sister, Diane. Bill was survived by his third wife of about thirty years, Elaine, and her four daughters and one son. Bill had known Elaine and her husband, George, many years ago when Bill's relationship with his second wife, Terry, went south. It was about the time that Elaine's husband George had passed away. Bill and Elaine (pictured right) got together, got married, and spent the rest of their lives together. Sadly, Elaine passed away November 9, 2009, at the age of seventy-six. Both Bill and Elaine are buried in a cemetery in Northeast

Philadelphia. Keep in mind that Walter acquired the house at 42 Rolling Lane in Levittown because Bill and his first wife, Betty, were breaking up and neither one wanted the house. Betty (pictured left), who was born on January 6, 1933, died after a lengthy illness October 8, 2012. I mention Betty because I had the opportunity to tell her about my desire to roll in the hay with her when I was young boy, and I'm sure I made her day. Betty was downright beautiful up to the very end.

* * *

Eleanor Ann Cunningham, the daughter of my brother Bob and his wife Eleanor, was the first niece to pass away. She was born September 20, 1955, and died, after fighting many different illnesses—for her entire married life, it seemed—on August 25, 2009, shy of her fifty-fourth birthday. She was married to John Cunningham, who was born December 26, 1955, and died June 18, 2012, after a long illness. Eleanor Ann became a registered nurse at a very young age. Her husband John was a security expert in retail stores. Bob and El also had two sons, Bobby and John.

Bob and El met and got married when they were very young and in the Navy; my brother Bob was just eighteen. Bob was a truck driver and worked for Fox Transport and then Trans-Con his entire adult life. Eleanor was a teacher who taught from first to eighth grade in the Bristol Township School

District for her entire life. She was also a lay minister with the Methodist Church. Bob and Eleanor celebrated their sixtieth wedding anniversary prior to her death on December 25, 2012.

* * *

It was at my brother Bob and his wife Eleanor's fiftieth wedding anniversary celebration that my sister-in-law Barbara informed the family that my brother Ted had officially been diagnosed with Alzheimer's disease. Ted was sixty-one years old. My wife Mary had suspicions concerning Ted's memory. At times when Ted was working with me, he'd forget to lock the doors or forget what he was doing. It became so bad that my godson Brian would pick him up in the morning and take him home at night. Everyone was concerned, especially Ted's wife Barbara, that he might get lost or forget his way home. This was only after he did forget his way home once, but everyone blew it off as not a big deal.

When we first moved to Shamong, I realized just how close Ted and Barbara lived with their two sons, Joe and Dave. This is the same Dave that, as of this writing in May 2014, has been working with me twenty-four years. Ted had recently been discharged from the United States Marine Corps after serving almost twenty years. He worked third shift as a dispatcher at a trucking company. Fortunately for

me, this trucking outfit was very close to one of my main suppliers of plywood and laminate. So rather than wait for my delivery date, I would call and ask Ted to stop and pick up supplies. Gradually he also started to help me in building my cabinets and countertops. This was only a few hours in the morning. Sometimes, if I had worked

all night on rush orders, I would sleep in the truck as Ted would drive to the jobsite. Ted did not want to be put on the payroll, so in lieu of a paycheck, I bought him a new Ford pickup truck to pick up supplies. This was the same brother who, when I was in boot camp, came to camp Lejeune and took me out for liberty. I cherish the moments that we spent together in the mornings, getting to know one another better. Frankly, Ted was the only person with whom I ever discussed my leaving the Marine Corps, and honestly, he agreed with my decision. This was very important to me because I had the utmost love and respect for Ted.

Ted worked with me for another five years, one day a week. But his condition became so bad that Barbara made the decision that it would better for Ted if he no longer worked with us. She was right. Ted lived for another five years. His last three years were in a nursing home, and for the most part, he didn't recognize anyone. In those three years, I never went to see him. Before their deaths, I saw Walter and Donny deteriorate into people I didn't recognize. Instead of having the memory of Walter and Donny in their prime, I remember them sick and dying. I don't remember Ted that way. I remember him as he was. I'm glad I made the decision I did. Ted was born on February 1, 1940, and died April 23, 2011. He was seventy-one years old, and I really do miss him.

* * *

On October 14, 2012, my former brother-in-law Walter Parkhurst died. I hate to use the term "former" because I still loved him, even though I hadn't seen him in almost fifty years. As young children living on Haverford Avenue, Baring Street, Belmont Avenue, and the first few years at Bartram Village, he and my sister Sophia (pictured right) were the only bit of class that my mother, my brothers Jackie and Donny, and I had. Usually he had a big smile, and as I remember, he laughed a lot and would always sneak the Reddi-wip can of whipped cream and give Jackie and me some right out of the can. He was always kind to us,

unless Mom asked him to be a disciplinarian. He was always kind to Mom. Sophia and he had one son, Gary. I wish I could say good things about Gary, but I would be lying. Unlike his father, Gary was self-centered concerning his mother; his wives, and that's plural; even his children. He made it a point to exclude his mother and her family from his life, so screw him. I've met one of his sons, Michael, and in my opinion, he is a stand-up guy. He includes his grandmother in everything. I only wish Gary was half the man his son Michael is.

Parkey (what my brothers and I called Walt) and my sister Sophia had a daughter named Lisa. She was only one year old when Sophia and Walt broke up, so for the most part, my sister Sophia brought up Lisa by herself. Lisa never did get to know Parkey.

Gary was about thirteen years old when the breakup occurred, and I think he blamed his mother for the breakup, which was totally wrong because Parkey had found himself a girlfriend and was unfaithful to Sophia. I know this broke her heart, and I believe she never stopped loving him, even after his death. I know Sophia struggled financially until Lisa was out of the house, but I never heard her complain about it. Other than Mary, my sister Sophia is the most important woman in my life, and my love for her grows every year that I get to know her and her old-fashioned values which, unfortunately, do not exist in society today.

* * *

I really don't know how to write about my brother Jackie, for he hasn't really had any deaths to deal with in his immediate family, other than his third wife Barbara's father, Vince. Jackie's first marriage to Tina didn't last that long. The only good thing to come out of it was his first daughter, Joanne, and their relationship didn't get good until she was an adult. His second wife, Lillian, gave him his second daughter, Michelle, my goddaughter. He also assumed the responsibility for raising Lillian's daughter Renée. Here again, the marriage did

not last. Jackie didn't get lucky until he met Barbara, the love of his life. They've been married about twenty-five years, and honestly, Jackie is happier than a pig in slop. This is true, I believe, because Jackie finally let God into his life.

Jackie was having chest pains and went to the doctor. The doctor, in turn, had Jackie take a stress test. The result was not good. Jackie immediately had a quadruple bypass and then went into the intensive care unit. Jackie told his friend Reds that it felt like an elephant on his chest. He really scared his friend Reds, who is an ordained deacon. He told Jackie that if he would accept Jesus Christ as his Savior that Reds was positive God would get him through his ordeal. Jackie agreed to it, and he did get through the operation, but with complications.

Jackie, being an honorable guy, kept his word. Both he and Barbara converted to Catholicism, and the only way that their marriage could be recognized by the Church was if Jackie's previous marriages were annulled. Jackie gave me the forms required by the Church and asked me to be honest in my opinion before I gave them directly to a priest, not to Jackie, which I did. I mention this because I told the priest what a real piece of crap Jackie had been prior to meeting Barbara. The priest told me that if Jackie were granted the annulments, it would probably be because my statements were helpful. Jackie's first marriages were not marriages made in heaven. Jackie did receive the annulments, and his and Barbara's marriage was recognized by the Church. Jackie and Barbara even went further and became Eucharistic ministers.

Jackie and Barbara bought a building lot in the historic section of Bristol, where they built a Victorian-style home completely approved by the historical society

in Bristol. Jackie was instrumental in every facet of the building of this home. When I think of Jackie and Barbara's home, I often think how far from Bartram Village and the projects we've come. Jackie still comes to the shop two days a week. I'm proud to call Jackie my brother, and I'm honored to call him my friend.

* * *

Throughout this chapter known as "Reflections," I've written about my siblings and their immediate families, and about my former father-in-law, Jack Newberg. Not to include my sister-in-law Josephine Montenaro Nobile, Mary's only sibling,  would be a grave injustice. I would be lying if I said that Joey and my relationship was good, because it wasn't. On the other hand, it wasn't hostile either, as far as I was concerned. She was Mary's sister and if Mary loved her, I did. Joey was different and that is said in a good way. She stayed in Bayonne too long after graduating from Jersey City State College as a teacher, but she could not get a job in the public school system. She turned to a Catholic school system and worked as a teacher in Bayonne. I think her college was wasted: she wasn't happy as a teacher. She went to work in a health-food store, and then went on to having her own store with her husband, Bruce. She then started an arts-and-crafts business, which required her to work her ass off with very little return. I always felt bad for her. Joey seemed to be afraid of everything, and I don't think she trusted very many people. I am sensitive to this because Mary also seems to have some of the same tendencies.

When I said she stayed too long in Bayonne, I mean exposed to her father and his idiosyncrasies. I never did feel comfortable around him. Mary and Josephine could not have loved one another more. Josephine died on Friday the 13th of August 2010 in Samaritan Hospice in Mount Holly. Josephine was born February 10, 1953. She was fifty-seven years old at the time of her death. She barely lived longer than Nellie, her mother, who died at the age of fifty-four.

As I mentioned, Josephine was afraid of everything and everyone. In my opinion, at the top of her list was not to trust, and to fear, doctors. I bring this up for a reason. When she was first diagnosed with a tumor in her brain, she was told that she had three months to live. She was told the tumor was inoperable.

I don't think she would've let them operate anyway. My understanding is that she told her husband Bruce and her sister Mary that she did not want doctors to cut into her. The doctors got to her husband, and he allowed them to drill into her skull and give her radiation therapy. It didn't work, and she only lived for six weeks from the time of being diagnosed. I guess the doctors were wrong or the therapy was harmful, and she never regained her alertness. When I questioned Mary about this decision, she told me it was Bruce's decision and not hers, and that I should stay out of it. On the morning Josephine died, Mary called me with the bad news. Knowing that one of Josephine's last wishes, and perhaps her most important wish, was to be interred within twenty-four hours of death, immediately after Mary and I hung up, I called the undertaker and pushed him to make this happen, and he accommodated her wish.

Years earlier, Mary and Josephine had purchased five cemetery plots next to one another at Sacred Heart Cemetery, the Catholic cemetery in Mount Holly. The five plots were for Josephine and Bruce, Mary and me, and my father-in-law Jimmy. I bring this up because my father-in-law died first. Without thinking, he was buried in the middle plot. Consequently, when Josephine died, they put her next to Jimmy, leaving Bruce to be buried on one end, and Mary and me on the other side of Jimmy. Mary and Josephine wanted to be buried next to one another, but with the arrangement at the cemetery as it is now, that will be impossible because Bruce would also be buried next to Josephine. So if Mary precedes me in death, I'm going to have Jimmy dug up and moved to one end.

As I said, Josephine seemed to fear everything and didn't trust easily. I can say this knowing I'm absolutely right that Josephine put all her trust in Jesus Christ. She was one of the most pious people I've ever met. She attended Mass daily and gave to the Church, which she didn't have. She always had my utmost respect when it came to faith. I know she and my mother-in-law Nellie are in heaven, looking down and guiding Mary.

CHAPTER 14

The Program

I'M NOT SURE WHEN IT happened, or when I developed my alcoholism. I don't think anyone knows.

As a youth in the projects, we would bribe a bum or wino to get a bottle of Thunderbird or some other cheap wine. As I saw it, it was a rite of passage for all young men to at least experiment. I really didn't enjoy the wine and never developed any kind of a taste for it, even as a teenager drinking at Jimmy Cook's house. I just didn't enjoy it. In the Marine Corps, drinking would've gotten me into a whole lot of trouble, so I decided against it. Not even as a young man did I enjoy drinking. When I was a district manager with Morse Shoe, occasionally I would drink too much at dinner, but it really wasn't a problem. If I got drunk and was pulled over by the police, the police would ask me if I was able to get home. Naturally, I always said yes. I was never even cited in any way for drunk driving. While working with Harry Bagot at the management company, I would occasionally stop, on Fridays after work, for happy hour at a place across the street from the Cherry Hill office. But again, this wasn't a problem. Up to this point, I didn't even enjoy beer.

I guess it was when I first went into business. I remodeled a bar known as the Towne Tavern in Riverside. There was no running water in this tavern, but there was plenty of beer, and I acquired a taste for beer. At that point it still wasn't a problem, up to our move to Shamong. That first year in Shamong, when I worked by myself, I think the problem started. I started having beer and liquor delivered to our home when Mary wasn't there. I even developed a taste for hot beer and liquor, because I didn't have a refrigerator in my shop at home, and I didn't want Mary to see how much I was actually drinking. There were times when I only left the driveway two or three times the entire week, to go to Mass and maybe install a kitchen or two. Mary was leaving the house very early in the morning to go to work. I couldn't drink that much coffee. It made me shake, and I never had a sweet tooth, so soda pop or sweet drinks were out of the question. Beer was just right.

It took a few years of drinking beer from 7 a.m. until just before Mary got home from work for the problem to start to be out of hand. I think that at first she didn't pay any attention to it, but she soon learned that a problem was developing. It was after the death of my brother Walter that Mary observed my increased drinking. After the death of my brother Donny, it got much worse. Somewhere in that time, I started drinking vodka at about 11 a.m. Honestly, I was half drunk all the time. It was no longer an option for me to go out and drive. I was terrified that I would hurt someone or hurt myself. By this time I had started my car collection, and I didn't want to hurt any of them either.

One Saturday in August in the year 2000, Mary asked me if I would have only one drink for the day so I wouldn't be slurring my words or staggering when we went out to dinner. I told her that would not be a problem. That Saturday, I had one drink and said screw it and proceeded to drink more. The following day, I thought it was rather strange that I'd continued to drink after the first one, so I said to myself that the following week I would try it again. Unfortunately, the result was the same. A light went on in my head, and I thought there was something wrong. At that time, I had no idea what an alcoholic was. I found it awfully hard to believe that I could not have one drink and stop. With this in mind, I decided I would give up drinking as a New Year's resolution or for Lent and not start again. But in the meantime, I was going to get my full share of alcohol in the last four months of the year.

I'm ashamed to say that I really started drinking. I was drunk all the time. I had to have a drink in the morning to shake off the hangover. The only time I didn't drink was before I went to Mass. I had a lot of respect for the Church. It was my habit to give up drinking for Lent, but in the year 2000, I didn't. A lightbulb should have gone off in my head, but it didn't. By the way, Lent is not forty days: it's forty-seven. I used to have a countdown and stay up on Easter Saturday so I could drink after midnight again. Even with this in mind, I did not think that I had a problem. I thought I just liked to drink a lot.

My relationship with Mary was strained more than it ever had been. I believe it was in November that Mary left. It took me two weeks to realize that she was gone. The only way I was sure that she was gone was that half the pictures on our "dead table" were gone. Our dead table was a table with pictures of people who had passed away whom both Mary and I had loved. I knew that they didn't just get up and walk away. The period between Thanksgiving and Christmas was merely a blur and was by far the worst holiday I'd ever had, including when I was a child. I woke up the day after Christmas and spoke with God. I asked him to have my soul rot in hell should I ever drink again. I didn't want to be forgiven for drinking. I just wanted to stop drinking. This was not the conventional way to stop drinking, but it was my way. I had no intention of going to rehab or anything of that nature.

I decided I would stay home and get past the shakes, which I learned were the DT's. On the sixth day of being sober, an explosion went off in my head. I had no idea what it was. I was soon to find out that I'd had a stroke. This was my first stroke. It was a very mild stroke, but it was a stroke. My doctor was on vacation and his fill-in prescribed narcotics to calm me down. Naturally, I didn't take them. When my doctor came back, he really laid out the fill-in doctor for doing such a stupid thing. My doctor and I agreed that I already had a problem with alcohol, and I shouldn't replace it with drugs. By the grace of God, I have no lasting effects from the first stroke, nor from the second stroke, which took place over two years later.

Not having Mary with me over the holidays made me realize just how much of my life she had become. We had been married thirty years at that point, and whatever I would have to do to get her back, I was going to do.

She was staying at her sister's house, and it was easy for them to let the answering machine pick up the phone when I called, to avoid having to talk with me. My other option was to reach her where she had recently started a new job. It had been three years since she had worked, and she was getting downright bored being home. She decided to get a full-time job. Mary would never air her problems with anyone, so I would call her at her office knowing for sure she would take my call. After I almost became a nuisance to the telephone operator at her office, she finally accepted my call. She made it quite clear that she would not live with or stay married to an alcoholic, and frankly, it took me a while to convince her to meet with me, and even then she would only meet at the rectory of St. Mary of the Lakes church together with Father Tedesco, the parish rector. He agreed with Mary that no one should have to be married to an alcoholic. At this stage of my life, I also agree with that belief.

Father Tedesco suggested that Mary and I meet with a marriage counselor. Her name was Maryann. Mary and I made an appointment with her and met with her jointly and then individually. She asked Mary to come back again a few times. I never knew why and I never asked. Maryann's advice to me was to go to rehab. I expressed that I would never go to rehab; frankly, because I didn't want this to appear on my medical history. Her other suggestion was that I get involved in a 12-step program. She gave me no idea what the program was. My conception of a 12-step program was a group of men that slept in cardboard boxes, had no job, and lived under bridges for protection. I could not have been more wrong.

My first call to the program was on a Monday morning, and I was informed that there was a meeting being held at eight at Cathedral of the Woods in Medford Lakes, New Jersey, that same evening. This was the first meeting I was to attend in the program. I really didn't like it very much. It was a mixed meeting of men and women, and it seemed that everyone was happy except me. When people spoke, it was referred to as a sharing. I had no idea what they were talking about, maybe because most of the people that shared were women. I'm not sure if it's what they were saying, or maybe I was less than overjoyed to be there. It seemed everyone was concerned about a woman who'd obviously had a little time sober, and who then had gotten drunk and decided to come back to the program. I did recognize one person that I knew. I also learned that last names were never used anymore. We used initials only. This makes it very hard when you need someone's phone number, or when they're hospitalized. It's very hard to find out what room they're in.

I will call him "Tom W." Tom W. and I had done business in the past. I had built him a kitchen for his home. He, in turn, had done some brickwork on my deck and built a stone flower bed on the lake. I think Tom had two years sober when I first saw him at a meeting. I also met Paul D. He lived in Indian Mills, New Jersey, about two miles from my home, and he was without a driver's license. I mentioned to him after the meeting that I intended to go to another meeting the following evening. He asked me if I would mind picking him up for that meeting, because he really liked the Tuesday-night men's meeting. Paul shared with me that he had lost his driver's license for ten years due to a third DWI (driving while intoxicated). I believe Paul had already had three years without a driver's license. Paul and I would ride together for the next three years, even after he got his driver's license back. (He found a good lawyer who found a loophole that permitted him to get his driver's license back.) He'd pick me up occasionally. Paul lived at home with his mom and stepfather. He was kind of footloose and fancy-free. I got to know Paul's mother, and I know she was proud that she lived to see Paul get and stay sober. Unfortunately, she passed away three years after I got sober. I got to know Paul's fiancée, soon to be wife, and his children. I'm pleased to say that Paul is still sober at the time of this writing. He has been sober for sixteen years.

After that first meeting, I honestly had doubts as to whether the program was the route for me. Needless to say, I did pick Paul up and attended the Tuesday-night men's meeting. It started out just as boring as the Monday-night meeting I'd gone to until I heard Jimmy B. share. Jimmy was in his late sixties the first time I met him. When he spoke, he made things so simple to understand, and I truly enjoyed listening to him. I would learn later on that Jimmy had sponsored a number of people, and he had over twenty years sober at the time of my first meeting. I also feel honored to have considered Jimmy a friend. When you had questions about anything in the program or life, you could call Jimmy and he'd give you a straight, honest answer with no bullshit. I remained friends with Jimmy until his death in 2012. Jimmy, in my opinion, was a solid 12-step-program guy and a stand-up individual. A true testament to how highly Jimmy was thought of was that at his funeral services, there were over nine hundred people in attendance.

Right after Jimmy shared, the next person to share was Ray H. Whatever Jimmy left out, Ray picked up on and put in. When Ray shared, it sounded to me as if he were talking about my life, and in a roundabout way, he advised me as to what I should do without being that direct. At that first meeting, Ray helped me with at least three different problems. I learned at that meeting that whenever Ray spoke, I should listen and I still do. He has a way of making things so simple and right to the point without being obvious. Unfortunately, I don't think Ray wanted to develop a friendship with me up front, and I think I know the reason why. In Vietnam no one wanted to know the FNG (fuc*ing new guy). If you got to know that person and he got killed, a little bit of you was killed with him. In the program, if a new person comes in and you get to know them and they're not successful in obtaining long-term sobriety, it saddens you greatly. In the program, unlike most other organizations or businesses, even if you don't like the person, you still root for them to be successful in obtaining permanent sobriety.

I would later find out that Jimmy was Ray's winter sponsor. I was fifty-three when I came into the program. In the year 2000, Ray was in his late sixties and had eight years sober. At that time, Ray wasn't really that friendly until Mary and I met him and his wife Kelly at the 7:30 a.m. Mass at St. Mary of the Lakes. A few months later, after I had seen Ray and Kelly at Mass every Sunday, I decided to ask them to have breakfast with Mary and me at the Lite Bite Restaurant in Medford, New Jersey, after Mass one Sunday. I learned at breakfast that Kelly was also in the program. She and Ray had met in the program. She had a little less time sober than Ray. Ray and Kelly would become good friends to Mary and me, and we would have dinner together every few months or so.

I would also find out that Ray was one of the funniest men I'd ever met in my life. Along with his military experience in Germany, he was also the oldest bookie in Philadelphia. He owned a bar on Kensington Avenue in the Kensington section of Philadelphia, and if anyone should write a book, it is Ray. I've told him that many times. Unfortunately, Kelly was diagnosed with cancer in September 2011 and passed away in December 2011. Kelly was Ray's third wife. They had been married for fifteen years.

Ray's first marriage was quite similar to my first marriage. Both Ray and I were too young and did the honorable thing. I'm not sure, but I think Ray was drunk when he married his second wife. When Kelly died, Ray was devastated. He never realized exactly what he had. Unfortunately, I believe that is the situation with most people. They don't know what they have until they lose it. After a few years of mourning, Ray did develop a relationship with Barbara, a woman he had known for a good number of years, and honestly, they are the most fun people to be with. It's like they have been with one another their entire lives. I believe Ray's ethnicity is German, but he had the luck of the Irish, with two women, the first being Kelly. She was an uptown, classy woman who was probably too good for Ray. The second woman in his life is Barbara. I think she wanted to be an interior designer, a construction worker, and a boxer. She is one of the most beautiful women I know. Ray has breakfast with Mary and me every Sunday after Mass, and I have dinner with Ray and a few other fellas from the program every Tuesday. Ray has become one of my very best friends.

Ray's best friend, I think, is Barbara; his second-best friend is Eddie M. Putting Eddie and Ray together is a constant laugh. They have been friends since grammar school, and they're both in their late seventies and look like they're in their fifties. When I came into the program, Eddie was Ray's summer sponsor. The reason for this is that Eddie used to spend three months in Florida every winter, and several years ago Eddie and his wife Carmela bought a condominium outside of Fort Lauderdale, Florida, and now they spend six months a year there. Since the passing of Jimmy B., Eddie has become a long-distance, full-time sponsor to Ray.

I think it's about time I explained what a sponsor is in the program. It is a person who kind of guides you through the program. It's a person whom you can tell anything to, and who will, hopefully, give you good advice. It is believed that if you follow the Twelve Steps of the program you have a very good chance of obtaining lifelong sobriety. Your sponsor helps you to understand the Twelve Steps. It is somewhat complicated and every sponsor is somewhat different. I chose not to have a sponsor when I first came into the program. I believed then, and I believe now, that my Lord and Savior is my sponsor, and I can speak to him anytime I like. Due to this decision, I'm not qualified to sponsor anyone, though I've been asked many times. I mention this because I think Eddie was my sponsor and I didn't know it, because in my first year in the program, when Eddie was back from Florida, he spent just about every day with me, and frankly, he was a great help. He clarified many things in the program. I've always taken things literally. The program is not literal. Eddie, like Jimmy B., did sponsor a number of people. That is one of the steps in our 12-step program, which states that we help other alcoholics achieve sobriety. Eddie, in fact, is one of the most solid program guys I know.

Eddie was the former president of the local Teamsters union, and has been retired for a good number of years. Eddie is a shining example of how one should look after oneself in the area of health. I understand that he is afflicted with challenges that require him to live a disciplined life, and he follows the rules. Eddie and Carmela had three daughters and four sons. They also took on the responsibility of raising Eddie's niece and nephew. People like Eddie and Carmela, other than their political beliefs, are what our nation should be full of. They are honest, sincere, responsible, and respectful. I'm still amazed that Eddie and I are still great friends in spite of the fact that we're at completely opposite ends politically. Eddie is to the left and somewhat liberal, whereas I am to the right—actually, to the right of Genghis Khan.

These three men would go on to become the foundation of my membership in the program, and thinking back at this point, I would be pretty hard-pressed to find three men better qualified.

It is suggested that new people, referred to as "newcomers," attend ninety meetings in ninety days. In my case, this was completely out of the question. Keep in mind that I'd had a slight stroke, and I hadn't come back all the way. I was exhausted all the time, and I'm not sure it was due to the stroke or that feeling that overcomes just about everyone when they first get sober. I still functioned, but if you knocked on the door, there was no one home inside. I wasn't happy. I wasn't sad. I was just not at home. That's the only way I can express the feeling. This feeling continued for the first six months or so that I was sober. I'm told that alcohol causes the pituitary gland, located at the base of the brain, to stop producing endorphins. I'm also told that endorphins cause one to feel well, and it generally takes a little while for the pituitary gland to start working again. After the first six months, I kept getting better and better, but my energy wasn't coming back. I even moved a cot to my office so I could take a nap several times during the day. With this in mind, I attended three meetings a week for the first month, then two meetings a week for three months, and I've been going to one meeting a week ever since. I have attended more than one meeting a week on certain occasions when people have asked me, for many different reasons.

When I first came into the program, I really had a problem with a concept that is widely used in the program, and that is "one day at a time." Just about my entire adult life, I've had to plan ahead: next day, next week, next month, next year, and many years in advance. I had a problem with this until I met a woman by the name of Annie. The way she explained it to me was clear and concise: one day at a time dealing with my addiction. Most people in the program consider alcoholism a disease. I do not agree with that. I abused alcohol and became addicted to it. As I see it, a disease is something you have no control over. Again as I see it, it's an excuse. I don't need any excuses like "it wasn't my fault." My addiction was my own fault.

One of the fundamental aspects of the program is the Twelve Steps. These steps, I understand, were written by Bill W. and Dr. Bob in the 1930s. Those were the men who proved that one sober alcoholic has the best chance of helping another alcoholic, and the first thing that we must admit is Step 1. That step and the other eleven steps are:

1. We admitted we were powerless over alcohol—that our lives had become unmanageable.
2. Came to believe that a Power greater than ourselves could restore us to sanity.
3. Made a decision to turn our will and our lives over to the care of God, as we understood Him.
4. Made a searching and fearless moral inventory of ourselves.
5. Admitted to God, to ourselves, and to another human being the exact nature of our wrongs.
6. We were entirely ready to have God remove all these defects of character.
7. Humbly ask Him to remove our shortcomings.
8. Made a list of all the persons we had harmed, and became willing to make amends to them all.
9. Made direct amends to such people wherever possible, except when to do so would injure them or others.
10. Continued to take personal inventory and when we were wrong, promptly admitted it.
11. Sought through prayer and meditation to improve our conscious contact with God, as we understood Him, praying only for knowledge of His will for us and the power to carry that out.
12. Having had a spiritual awakening as a result of these Steps, we tried to carry this message to alcoholics, and to practice these principles in all our affairs.

In addition to the steps, service is suggested. Service as a greeter at meetings, as the person who chairs the meeting, as a person who makes the coffee, as someone who sets up the chairs or cleans up after the meeting, as a sponsor of other people, even as far as giving rides to other alcoholics—basically, anything that helps the group or an individual in or outside the program. At the time of this writing, I have been answering the phone for the program, two hours a week for the last eleven years.

One of the first things I learned in the program was honesty, and I learned that honesty starts with me. In my opinion, without honesty I had no chance of obtaining my goal, and the goal of all honest alcoholics, to stay sober permanently. I had to look at my life and see what I had become. Honestly, only by being honest with myself could I start to forgive myself. This was not easy, but I found that as I learned to like the man in the mirror, my life started getting better and better. It got to where Mary would take advantage of my honesty and ask me questions that I couldn't get out of or change the subject. I did learn that the answer is always the same: When you're honest, the answer never changes.

The Tuesday-night men's meeting that I was attending always had three topics of discussion, and the first was always: "Did you want to drink today?" The second and third topics changed weekly. Every time I shared, I had to answer that first question in the affirmative, honestly, for the first three years, because I did want to drink, and by the grace of God and the fellowship of the program, I didn't. I think my obsession lasted as long as it did because I didn't and couldn't use the program to its fullest extent. There were people who came into the program after me who lost the obsession long before I did. I can remember thinking and saying to myself that I must be chopped liver; when was the obsession going to leave? I recall very distinctly when it ended. I started to share at the Tuesday-night men's meeting, and I realized I didn't think about drinking until I started to share. Within a few weeks, I stopped thinking about it altogether, and have never thought about it again. I was under the impression that I had the record, and then I met Eddie D. Eddie had a lot of years sober, and he told me it was five years that he thought about it. I must say, though, since I've been sober, many new flavored alcoholic beverages have been on the market, and I do wonder how they taste.

Another important thing that I learned was that the program was spiritual. They would never talk directly about God, but that's exactly what I interpreted a higher power of being to be. This is where I had one leg up. I was always spiritual and have strong faith in my higher power, which I choose to call Jesus Christ. I was somewhat ashamed of how strong my faith was. It wasn't polite to be getting shit-faced and talking about God, or at least that's what I felt. Now I could freely express my faith in God, with no embarrassment or shame. My favorite word begins with F and ends with K, and some people call it a bomb, but I truly believe that my God has no problem with that word as long as I don't take his name in vain and I have not committed any sin.

At the time I first got sober, I was attending 7:30 a.m. Mass at St. Mary of the Lakes church in Medford. For at least twelve years I'd been an usher, and never had I noticed that at least three other men from the Tuesday-night men's meeting also attended the same Mass. In addition to Ray and his wife Kelly, there were Steve W. and Phil G. Not only was Phil G. a doctor, but he is also included as one of the most pious men that I know. When I first met Phil, he had been sober for about thirteen years. Phil not only talks the talk, but walks the walk. I consider him a very good friend. As a matter of fact, currently Ray, Phil, Eddie M., John, and Rick S. meet for dinner every Tuesday night, not necessarily for the food but for the company.

Ray is John's sponsor and has been sober for about the last two years, since John came back from Florida. John had thirteen or fourteen years sober and, for one reason or another, decided he thought he could drink again. John would be the first to admit that he can't, because it took him a few years to get back into the program. I bring this up for one reason. When John shares, he shares from the heart, and he is one of the most honest people I know. In addition, he can explain in detail what alcohol has done to his life, and what he gave up when he gave up his thirteen or fourteen years of sobriety. People outside the program, I think, don't understand how helpful this is to people who are recently sober. I also consider John a good friend.

Rick S. is recently sober at the time of this writing. He has about ninety-six days sober. He's been trying for thirty years to attain permanent sobriety, and I believe that the best influence on a person who is struggling with alcohol is people with a lot of time sober. I currently pray that he remains sober, because he really is a good guy.

I'd been sober about three years when a new fella came into the program, Terry O. Terry and I had a lot in common, since both of us served in the United States Marine Corps. Terry was without a driver's license, and ironically, it was not due to a DWI, even though he was an alcoholic. He never got a DWI. He just drove real poorly. I used to pick Terry up for the Tuesday-night meeting. This went on for a few years until one day he drove to my shop and informed me that he'd gotten his driver's license back. He then told me that when his license was taken away, the judge would not tell him how long the suspension would be, and he told Terry not to call to try to find out. Terry has just about eleven years sober, and I hope his friendship with me has helped him to stay sober. This is just another example of the wreckage we leave behind when we get sober, and I really don't miss that havoc.

Writing about the program would not be complete if I did not include Norman C., the "real alcoholic," as he would call himself. Norman was one of the most honest people I knew. Among the things he shared was that he feared that he might outlive his money. Another situation was when his wife Linda was retiring: how his life would change after she retired. Norman's life did change all for the best because Norman, like me, married well above his station in life. I was saddened about his passing in December 2011. I truly miss his sense of friendship.

I had been sober about six or seven years when Tony R. came into my life. Tony and I were a lot alike. As people would say, we were a little rough around the edges. I met him at the Tuesday-night men's meeting. Tony had been trying to get sober for three decades. He would have a little time sober and then get drunk. Tony possessed many talents: auto mechanics, plumbing, and electricity to mention a few. Frankly, you name it, Tony could do it, except up to that point, he couldn't stop drinking. I think Tony was ticketed numerous times for driving while intoxicated. According to him, he was issued two DWIs in one week. It took a while, but I would come to learn that Tony lost his license for twenty-three years. At the point in time when I met Tony, it had been twelve years since he had driven. Tony was a year older than I, and we had many things in common. Tony served in the Army about the same time I was in the Marine Corps. Tony got married a year before I got married. Where we differed was that Tony started drinking very early in life and didn't stop.

Sometimes I would pick Tony up just so he would have something to do during the day. Without a driver's license, living in Medford was difficult at best. I'd bring him to our shop or to my house. Sometimes I let him drive a car in our parking lot. This really made his day, since he loved driving. In addition to the lack of a driver's license, Tony was afflicted with many different illnesses, among which was cancer. He would not stop smoking either. His wife, Sandy, would chauffeur him from doctor to doctor while maintaining a full-time job as a real estate salesperson and a part-time job as a hairdresser. I would later find out that she was the breadwinner in the household. Tony had asked me to be his sponsor when I first met him, but again, if I didn't have a sponsor, I couldn't be a sponsor in the program. Therefore, I declined, but just as Eddie was my sponsor and I didn't know it, I was Tony's sponsor and he didn't know it.

It seemed that Tony was sick all the time and was constantly being hospitalized. When they built the new Virtua hospital on Route 73 in Voorhees, New Jersey, I told Tony he should go down and tell the developers what color he wanted his room painted, he was there so often. Tony also had a good sense of humor. I don't mean to talk out of school, but Tony's doctors advised him that there was a need to operate on his digestive system, which would necessitate his wearing a bag. He was totally against it, but to appease others, he consented to it. He was told by the doctors that they would later reverse the process and eliminate the bag. I believe that was to be twelve weeks after the operation. Then the doctors started to include other stipulations for reversal, which Tony couldn't achieve.

It was at this point that Tony shared with me that he would like to end it all and maybe commit suicide. Knowing that he held the same religious values I did, I reminded him of the consequences and suggested that he merely tell the doctors to reverse the procedure and eliminate the bag. Regardless of the outcome, and in my opinion, he would not be committing suicide after I gave him this advice. I brought this problem to my parish priest, and to my surprise, he agreed with my answer. Tony did force the doctor to reverse the operation and he did, in fact, die in October 2011. I know that because of our relationship, Tony stayed sober, for the most part, for the last three years of his life, and because he didn't take his own life, he had a great chance of meeting his Lord and Savior.

An interesting thing happened the day after his services. I, too, have health challenges, and on that day, I spent the day in bed. I never open the blinds, but on this particular day, I did. There is a rhododendron bush outside our bedroom, and there, in late October, I saw one gigantic blossom, and I know it was Tony. I really miss my friend, and hopefully, we will see each other in Paradise.

Getting back to Paul D.: We had been riding together about six months when Woody, the person who formally opened the meetings, asked Paul if he would open the meetings. Paul gladly accepted, and I guess I volunteered to make coffee. My role would go on for about four years, whereas Paul still opens the meetings today. He truly is a stand-up guy.

There are so many good people in the program, but I will never get this book finished if I don't stop writing about people in the program. I'm very comfortable in saying that, next to God, Mary, and my family, the program is the best thing that ever happened to me. The true and honest friends that I've found in the program make me glad that I'm an alcoholic and that I've had the opportunity to meet all these genuine people, men and women alike. One thing is constant in the program and that is honesty. It's such a joy to know that you're dealing with real people. I'd like to make one thing clear. The program did not get me sober, my God did. The program has taught me how to live sober, and it's a great way to live.

CHAPTER 15

Chelation Therapy: Is It Voodoo?

I'M LIVING PROOF THAT IT'S not. In previous chapters, I wrote of my two strokes. The second one was in February 2003. The only lasting effect of the second stroke was being exhausted. This was really interfering with my ability to work. I seemed to be tired all the time. Mary, naturally, shared this with her sister Josephine, who was really good at researching health matters. She'd had a thyroid operation and was not pleased with the results. Frankly, she never trusted any medical doctor again. Josephine started to believe strongly in homeopathic treatment, which included chelation therapy. Chelation therapy is when vitamins and minerals, among other things, are intravenously fed into your body.

After researching chelation therapy, Josephine came to the conclusion that the Cherry Hill Clinic was far superior to any other facility in the Marlton/Shamong area. She suggested to Mary that she make an appointment to meet Dr. Vijay (MD) and Dr. Molly Fantasia (PhD). Their office was in Cherry Hill. Dr. Vijay at that time was being treated for his diabetes and was not available. So Mary and I met with Dr. Molly Fantasia. I think to make us feel more at ease, she asked us to call her by her first name. Both Mary and I were very impressed with her. After speaking with her, she came up with a plan of attack on how to make me feel better. Initially, I started to go three times a week. Very quickly, it was reduced to twice a week and ultimately to once a week. Please note that my treatments were not covered by my insurance. Within the first few weeks, I started to feel better and stronger. But like every other human being on planet Earth, it wasn't fast enough.

Prior to my second stroke, one of my best friends, Michael Kloss, asked me to be his best man. Naturally, I said yes. Between the time that Michael asked me to be his best man and the wedding, I had my second stroke. He was marrying the love of his life, Kim. There were only two drawbacks. First, the wedding would take place in South Carolina. Interestingly enough, the wedding and reception would be at the location where the swamp scene from the motion picture *The Patriot*, starring Mel Gibson, was shot. It took every bit of energy I could muster to walk that half mile through the swamp. I only wish I had felt better and could've made a better best man at their reception, and made it into a more joyful time. If I had started chelation therapy prior to the wedding, I'm absolutely positive that I would've felt considerably better.

The second drawback was that I was there alone. Mary had to stay home and watch the dogs. I'd been sober about two years at that time, and I was well aware of the fact that there would be a lot of drinking. Michael and I had done a lot of drinking together in the past. He was the man who built my 1954 Ford, and I thought of him as a son. He was the only person with whom I had to limit my contact when I first got sober. This was something I really regretted, but I learned in the program that people, places, and things might cause some people to drink. I'm proud to say that I am the godfather of Mike and Kim's daughter Samantha. At the time of this writing, she is eighteen years old and a fine young lady, and she started college in the fall of 2014.

Getting back to chelation therapy, I think it worked so well because Dr. Molly Fantasia really does care, unlike many MDs I've known. She's always doing research and analyzing her treatment protocols. This lady is ranked among the greatest that I know, and I truly believe without her looking after me, I would not be alive today. Since Dr. Vijay was recovering from an episode with diabetes, his replacement, Dr. Veloso, was filling in as the MD in Molly's office. Dr. Veloso, as I would learn, was older than Dr. Vijay. Dr. Veloso was born in the Philippine Islands and practiced his entire life in the United States. When I met him, he was working part-time with Molly. When there were no other patients for Dr. Veloso to see, he would come and talk with me and the other patients while we received our treatment. This was something new for me, because I was fifty-six years old and had never had a relationship with a doctor who was treating me, where he didn't take on the godlike image. He was really down-to-earth, and he would fill in for Dr. Vijay more than once. I learned after his death in 2011 that he'd had a multitude of health challenges. I really liked and respected Dr. Veloso.

It was about four months after I started receiving chelation therapy that Dr. Vijay (pictured right) was well enough to return to the clinic. Dr. Vijay was born in India and practiced both in India, when he first became a doctor, and then in the United States on the West Coast. I bring this up because Dr. Vijay, as I understand it, was separated from his wife in California. I do believe that he still loved her very much, and that love might've cost him his life. Like Dr. Veloso, his head was not up his butt. He ranked up there with some of the smartest people I've ever known. He lived a very simple life and spent most of his time reading and keeping up with new medical things, but he failed to take care of his own health. In 2009 Dr. Vijay passed away due to complications from his diabetes. I truly miss his wit.

Speaking of intelligent people, I'd have to include two other people. First would be my friend Jim Pollum. I've known Jim since 1987. He was formerly the owner of several multifamily properties in Pennsylvania, and Kruger Kitchens, my company, supplied and installed cabinets for him and his wife Paula. I didn't know Jim well until 1999, when he attended and brought his girlfriend, soon-to-be wife, Cindy to our Fourth of July party. His ex-wife Paula, as I would learn, had developed a relationship over the Internet with another man, and according to Jim, she forced Jim to go out of business. I would learn that most of the properties were mortgaged and that Paula had some interest in the properties, and their breakup was not congenial. Jim, as I would learn, was extremely capable in the area of computers. To this day, he amazes me with the speed with which he works on programs. If I ever have a problem, I call him up and he walks me through the problem over the phone, for the most part. He started a company related to computers, security, and entertainment. He and Cindy purchased a home in Mount Holly, where they currently live. As with many other people, I'm proud to call Jim my friend.

In the winter of 1988–89, when Mary and I first moved to Shamong, the lake we live on was frozen. I saw two basset hounds out on the ice. I called our township's offices and inquired who owned the house and dogs. I found out that Stan Drinkwater was the owner. The township told me that he was an attorney in the city of Lindenwold, New Jersey. I called him and told him of the situation. He thanked me and informed me that there was an invisible fence which kept the dogs in, and there must've been something with the ice that caused the dogs to be able to go through the fence. He came home and retrieved his dogs, because they were large and the ice was not that thick.

Stan is not the typical lawyer. He's loyal, honest, compassionate, humble, and a real honorable man. He and I have been the best of friends since the winter of 1989. I've learned that Stan initially attended medical school, but decided to be a lawyer instead. He is versed in so many areas, and when he gets talking, he loses me quickly. He is that detail-oriented, and he attempts to explain everything from A to Z. About twenty years ago he moved to Atco, New Jersey, into a very old house that had a history as one of the stops on the Underground Railroad prior to the Civil War. It seemed he always has to do something around the house. I believe he truly misses the house on the lake. I value his friendship, his wisdom, and his advice.

Several years back, I introduced Stan to my really good friend Harry Bagot. They became immediate friends. As a matter of fact, Stan has had this idea of converting (the only word I know for it is) junk into energy. To this day, Stan and Harry are trying to get this company off the ground and listed on the New York Stock Exchange. It's been one royal pain in the ass.

Getting back to the Cherry Hill Clinic, I would be remiss if I failed to mention Molly's nurse, Lynda (pictured right). Lynda is a tall, beautiful, and well-qualified woman who has the patience of a saint. Recently, after twelve years of chelation therapy, my veins are becoming more and more difficult for her to find a vein into which to inject the chelation solution. She becomes so apologetic after two sticks, even though it's not her fault. At the time of this writing, Lynda has been a nurse for Molly for nineteen years.

I understand that Lynda was married years ago, but the marriage didn't work. I think she's currently gun-shy when it comes to marriage, even though I know she would make a perfect wife and companion. She has all the qualities that most men would gladly love to have her in their life. But in my opinion, the older we get, the more particular we become. It becomes easy to rule out contenders, but Lynda still has time, and I'll keep praying for her.

Last but not least in Molly's office is Barbara. Barbara is a retired registered nurse who has been with Molly since she retired. This woman really has her act together. She's probably forgotten more about homeopathic treatments than young students are taught. In addition to knowledge, she is also extremely efficient. Basically, nothing gets by her.

With Lynda and Barbara, Molly couldn't put together a better team based on knowledge, loyalty, and dependability.

Getting back to Molly (pictured above), an example of her true concern is when we have no option, due to my health challenges, but to see specialists. Under no circumstances will she let me go to appointments by myself, knowing of my distrust of doctors. To make my life easier, she's actually made trips to Baltimore to The

Johns Hopkins Hospital, in addition to several trips to Philadelphia to the Hospital of the University of Pennsylvania. She gives me her true, heartfelt reasoning as to whether or not to do something when we see a specialist. We represent her as my advocate, even though I would rather represent her as my sister. I would be proud to call her my sister. I do believe that without her in my life, I would've died years ago. One last thing: One of the highest compliments ever paid to me was from Molly, and that is when she told me that I am **my own man**.

CHAPTER 16
Conclusions

IN CONCLUSION, I CAN TRULY say that my life has been absolutely wonderful. I attained goals that were well beyond my wildest dreams. As an example, I remember telling my mother when I was a young boy that when I got older, I would buy her a nice television, and maybe an apartment not in the projects. That was the extent of my hopes and wishes. Maybe that was just the thinking of a young kid.

There were many people and events that helped shape my life. Most important was my mother; second was my brother Walter. I'm absolutely positive that without his intervention, Jackie, Donny, and I would've been criminals rather than the responsible individuals we've become. Walter must've seen something in us, and he set the groundwork for the future.

Having by far the greatest effect on my life has been my wife Mary. On September 20, 2014, Mary and I celebrated our forty-fourth wedding anniversary. We grew up together. We started as two individuals and became one. I've learned so much from her on how to be a man and be responsible. I'm sure she's learned from me as well. I know I couldn't have done better. She probably could have. I married up.

After writing this autobiography, I've learned that if I had to live my life over, I wouldn't have changed anything if it would have jeopardized my life with Mary. But on the other hand, if I could've changed things and not affected our relationship, there are four things I would have done differently:

1. I would never have quit high school. Even though I really hated it, I could've spent three years attending college, as opposed to spending three years at night high school.

2. I would've persevered in the Marine Corps and done exactly as they told me to do, because in my heart I am a patriot and I am proud to be an American living

in the United States of America. Unfortunately, the Johnson administration, in my opinion, felt the war was a game, and soldiers were merely pawns to achieve their political goals. Again in my opinion, he screwed up the war and really screwed up society with his Great Society program, which chased men out of their homes and the lives of their children.

3. I would never have married Sidra. To this day, damn near fifty years later, she still affects my life adversely. Assuming she was pregnant, I should've just agreed to pay support for the child.

4. Even though there were no DNA tests at that time, I would've had a blood test to determine, to some degree, whether or not I was the father of Stacy. Now I don't think I'll ever get the opportunity to request a DNA test from Stacy, even though I'm willing to pay for confirmation, one way or the other, of whether Stacy is related to me at all. I'm of the belief she's not, and frankly speaking, if I were to find out that she is my daughter, our relationship would not change in any way whatsoever. I understand she now has two children. I only learned about one, officially, from her, and that was when I last saw her for lunch (at the time of this writing, that was almost twelve years ago). And if it did prove true that I am Stacy's father, I would make sure to become a part of those two children's lives, and they would become a part of my life. Unfortunately, I don't believe Sidra would allow Stacy to agree to this.

Other than those four items, I view all life's experiences, good and bad, as tools of learning how to live my life, and I've tried to improve my life because of my experiences.

Relationships

I've learned in my sixty-seven years that one of the most important things in life is relationships—personal, business, political, and so on. As my mentor, Bert Actman, once said, "Friends are the most special people in life." Friendships start as relationships, and I've found that sharing things about my life first is the only way most people will open up and share things about their life. This was a very important lesson that I learned when I worked for Morse Shoe, and it works.

I also learned from Morse Shoe that personalities cannot be changed, but with a lot of practice, you can alter yours, hopefully for the better. I hope my changes have been for the better. I strongly believe that without good relationships, your life is lonely, boring, and dull, and your chances of being successful in business are limited.

A trait of my mother's that used to embarrass me was her straightforwardness. What used to be an embarrassment is now a welcome trait, as I see it. People have told me, in a complimentary way that I'm straightforward. I've been told that it's like a breath of fresh air to hear the same answer the same way all the time, and I try not to be offensive or hurtful to people, unless I want to be, but I know a basic rule. If a person thinks you offended them, whether you intended to or not, you did. I also feel that when I'm with anyone, and I do mean anyone, I must be aware of things I say and how they can be interpreted or misinterpreted by others. Honestly, you can never relax. That's what keeps life interesting.

Success in Marriage

Getting back to my life with Mary, I've often thought about why our marriage to this point has been successful. The only conclusion I can come to is that when we married, we didn't expect anything more than what we were then: a shoe department manager and a secretary. There were no hidden goals or future expectations. Neither one of us had the desire to change the other. I feel that in society today, newlyweds attempt to change their partner, which can and does lead to disaster. Though I can say, in the forty-four years we've been married, I've been married to six or seven different women, and frankly, some of them I didn't like very much. But the foundation of our marriage carried us through every rough spot.

Keep Them Laughing

I've learned that laughter is the elixir of life, above just about every other human attribute. In my opinion, someone could be rich, but if they're miserable and can't laugh, then they're poor. If someone is extremely intelligent but can't achieve a real belly laugh, then they're boring. I would even be bold enough to say that laughter lingers far longer than lust. Laughter should never be achieved at someone else's expense, unless you want it to be. If someone is humiliating someone else who doesn't have the ability to defend himself or herself, as a rule, my goal becomes to humiliate the abuser.

I really do believe "keep them laughing." I found you must first get people to laugh with you at yourself, then you can laugh with them at themselves. It always works. I've learned never to make it personal with people who are thin-skinned, unless they open the door.

Laughter has a way of breaking down barriers, such as when I answer the phone and people ask how I'm doing. I generally say, and I quote, "For an old man, I'm doing great," or "Thank God it's Friday," or "God, I wish this day was over," or "I'm glad to get out of this day [or week] with my life." This makes people laugh, and it gives me great joy to hear the laughter in their voice. It also helps to establish a personal relationship with whomever I'm speaking with. Just like common courtesy, laughter doesn't cost anything, except for a little thinking. I'm proud to say that after forty-four years, I still make Mary laugh, most of the time.

Changing Beliefs

I've always respected authority, but as I get older, I expect people in authority to earn my respect. The incompetence and abuse of people in authority gets under my skin, and I have no problem in exposing that misuse. Bureaucracy generally raises its ugly head when it comes to incompetence and abuse of authority. The most glaring example of this, in my opinion, is government, which also includes the court system.

For instance, the county expects two hundred people to show up for a fourteen-person jury (twelve jurors plus two alternates), and then we have less-than-competent people administering this procedure. I honestly think they have no idea or concern as to how much time and money they waste. Then to add insult to injury, the county will give you $5 to $10 per day to compensate you for showing up. The county then expects the employers to compensate all jurors, whether they're picked or not, for the difference. Assuming that only half of the jurors are employed, there still remain one hundred jurors for whom employers are expected to make up the difference in their pay. Assuming that the jurors earn $12.50 per hour for an eight-hour day, they would earn $100 per day. Subtracting the $10 a day the county pays each potential juror, the employers are expected to pay the one hundred jurors who work $90 per day. When multiplied by 100, that equals $9,000 a day or $45,000 a week or $2,340,000 per year to subsidize the incompetent and bureaucratic court system.

This could be resolved with professional jurors, who would be vetted prior to being employed. Or only use people who are receiving unemployment compensation, since they're getting paid already. This is so simple that I guarantee it will never happen.

Continuing on with the court system, the biggest abusers of authority, in my opinion, are judges. The difference between God and judges is that God doesn't think he's a judge. In my experience, 80 percent of judges are generally late to court, and they are downright condescending to defendants and to the prosecution as well, and their decisions confound the hell out of me. Could it be that they have an agenda that doesn't necessarily agree with the law? Other than term limits, I really don't know how to fix this.

Another example of abuse of authority is police, and county and state workers. A prime example of this is road construction: twenty county highway workers with trucks at one site, but only two men actually doing work. I find this to be an abuse of your and my tax dollars. Another example of abuse of authority is our school system, which graduates from the twelfth grade people who cannot read. There is no excuse for this. You add political correctness to bureaucracy and abuse of authority, and you really have a mess where no one is accountable. Last but not least is rudeness—from all aspects of government, including the police. I believe when you see rudeness directed at you, you have the right to be doubly rude to them, and I am.

Politics

Again, the older I get, the more Republican I become. All my life and since Mary has been married to me, I believe we've done what we thought was the right thing. We've worked hard and saved our money, never lived above are means, actually done without, and saved to buy things or do things. We've paid a bundle in taxes to state and federal government, including county school taxes, even though we've had no children. But I still say we did the right thing. Now that we are older, we're tired of paying those taxes. That brings me to Social Security. We were always told that it was "retirement," and I want all my money back, with interest.

I started paying Social Security taxes at the age of fourteen. I paid half and my employer paid half for twenty-four years. The last thirty years, I've paid both halves because I was self-employed and not on anyone's payroll, and I really do want my money back. For Social Security, as I see, is a true entitlement because we've paid for it. Another true entitlement is veterans' benefits. If you served honorably, veterans' benefits are a reward for your service to our country. I've already received VA benefits that enabled me to complete high school and attend college. The VA also helped Mary and me buy our first house by guaranteeing our mortgage and getting us a lower interest rate.

Other than accepting welfare as a child, I've never asked for, nor expected, any social programs to bail me out. As a matter of fact, I still view acceptance of social programs as a true embarrassment and something to be ashamed of. Only with this mind-set will social programs be minimized.

As I get older, I see our society changing, and not for the better. It seems everyone is trying to get into someone else's pocketbook. This is a direct result of politicians trying to get reelected using giveaways to get votes. The current administration in the White House is probably the best example of how people should not live their lives, spending well beyond their means. I believe all governmental agencies should be accountable to their constituents. It's not that I'm against social programs; I have personal experience, since Jackie, Donny, and I were on welfare when we were children, along with Mom. My father was a bum, and my mother couldn't pick a man. That left Jackie, Donny, and me at the mercy of the welfare department. It was a crappy childhood, but we ate and had a roof over our head. I committed, as a young boy, that once I was able to make it on my own, I would never accept charity.

As I see it, social programs are charity and the only people who should be taking advantage of social programs are women with children, when there are no men in their life. But it still should be something one should be ashamed of.

I think we would be better served by:

1. Imposing term limits. Too many politicians see serving in public office as career employment—for the money and the power. Term limits would also apply to all judges, including Supreme Court justices.

2. Instituting the line-item veto for all state and federal bills. All too often, a bill starts out good and then politicians start throwing pork into the bill. ("Pork," as I see it, is things that favor special groups or areas.) Hence, in order to get the good portion of the bill passed, the pork gets passed as well.

3. Eliminating lobbyists. As I see it, lobbyists are people who get paid to convince politicians to add pork, which favors companies or groups. I've learned that politicians take care of their friends through the tax code, establishing loopholes and things of that nature that are advantageous to their sponsors. Without lobbyists, these abuses could be reduced greatly.

4. Adding more general referenda at elections. This would take a great deal of authority away from the politicians, and not give them the chance to accomplish their personal agendas, and put it back where it belongs—in the hands of the general public. This would also prevent judges from setting policy. I would take away the ability of all courts, including the Supreme Court, to overturn the general public's mandate through public referenda.

As with most good suggestions, I'm not going to hold my breath waiting for these four items to be instituted.

* * *

What is the Difference Between Religion and Faith?

I once posed this question to a number of people. I often pose questions without leading to an answer, because I am truly looking for other people's opinions. The best definition was given by Molly's nurse, Lynda, and her answer was, and I quote, "Faith is the belief in a higher power. Religion is the way that one worships that higher power." I've always had faith and practiced religion.

When I was a child, Mom took Jackie, Donny, and me to a Lutheran Sunday school church at 47th and Kingsessing Avenue in Southwest Philadelphia. I believed as a child that God was this mean man in the sky who only punished people. That was really wrong. As I got older, I saw God as a friend, probably with a sense of humor. And I still do.

During the time that I drank, I was embarrassed to talk about God. Only when I gave up drinking did my spirituality grow to a point that I never thought I'd reach. I can truly say that I've gained peace in my life, and I don't fear death because I look forward to life in Paradise with my family and friends who have gone before me.

As far as religion goes, in my opinion, every religion is a compilation of man-made rules. I am a Catholic and I try very hard to practice my religion. Most of the time, I am successful. Sometimes I'm not. I truly believe all faiths—Gentile, Jew, Muslim, Hindu, and the others—pray to the same God. The conclusion I've come to is that religion is important but faith is more important, and I still pray for faith.

* * *

With my faith, my wife, my family and friends, I've attained happiness and fulfillment that surpassed all expectations of this white-trash kid from Southwest Philadelphia.

I thank you for taking the time to read my autobiography. To call myself an author is like calling the Red Cedar Hill Gang a "gang." What a joke. I really hope that I haven't bored you. I will close with one statement that I've stolen from a song sung by Frank Sinatra:

I Did It My Way!

One last thing: The opinions and interpretations are mine, with no malice intended against anyone.

SAYINGS AND BELIEFS

1. Get the cash.
2. Everybody lies.
3. They also exaggerate.
4. A dependable person becomes undependable when you depend on them.
5. No good deed ever goes unpunished.
6. There's nothing like a Lebanese deal; a Lebanese deal is where everyone gets screwed.
7. Don't be greedy: remember, PGS pigs get slaughtered.
8. Does your mother know you're an asshole?
9. As my mother would say, most people have sweet taste for shit.
10. Gratitude generally ends with "thank you"; to expect more is setting yourself up for disappointment.
11. Be grateful and don't be afraid to show it.
12. From my Marine Corps training: improvise, adapt, and overcome.
13. As my brother Walter would say, "Don't do as I do, do as I say."
14. As my brother Walter would say, "We'd rather have a sister in the whorehouse than a brother in the Army."
15. Learn the players and what positions they play, to play the game of life.
16. Learn the rules, then learn to circumvent them.
17. Don't get mad, get even.
18. As my mother would say, "He who loses his head, loses."

19. Always keep reserve money, time, and energy.

20. Never pay interest, if at all avoidable.

21. In the words of Joey Lewis, "A friend in need is a pest."

22. I'm not special.

23. By the grace of God go I.

24. Growing old is rough, but the alternative is much worse.

25. You'll get old—if you're lucky.

26. Never count on the government for anything; you will be sadly disappointed.

27. Stay well.

28. Every life is precious.

29. Trust in the Lord God only.

30. Let God in your life.

31. It is better to understand than it is to be understood.

32. One day at a time.

33. Find love and never let go.

34. You never find a new old friend.

35. Never lend what you cannot afford to lose.

36. Nothing ventured, nothing gained.

37. Be a stand-up guy.

38. Forgive, but never forget.

39. Some you win, some you lose, and some get rained out.

40. It's nice to be important, but it's more important to be nice.

41. Believe in women's intuition.

42. If you believe that, I will sell you a bridge.

43. A true friend is more concerned with your character than your comfort.

44. Don't mean nothin'.

45. When in doubt, SYA one—save your ass first.

46. My belief, impossible tasks done immediately; miracles take a little longer.

47. Hope for the best, prepare for the worst.

48. Always remember where you're from.

49. Never put on airs.

50. Follow the Golden Rule: Do unto others as you would have them do unto you.

51. Easy does it, don't overreact.

52. You must like the person in the mirror.

53. You can't make a silk purse from a sow's ear.

54. If everything seems to be going good, you've obviously overlooked something.

55. You can do nothing about yesterday. Yesterday is gone. You can do very little about today, but you can do a whole lot about tomorrow.

56. Never let success go to your head.

57. Keep them laughing.

58. Practice humility.

59. Pray for faith, for only through faith will you find peace.

60. Last but not least: My biggest weakness is also my greatest strength—an over-developed sense of urgency.

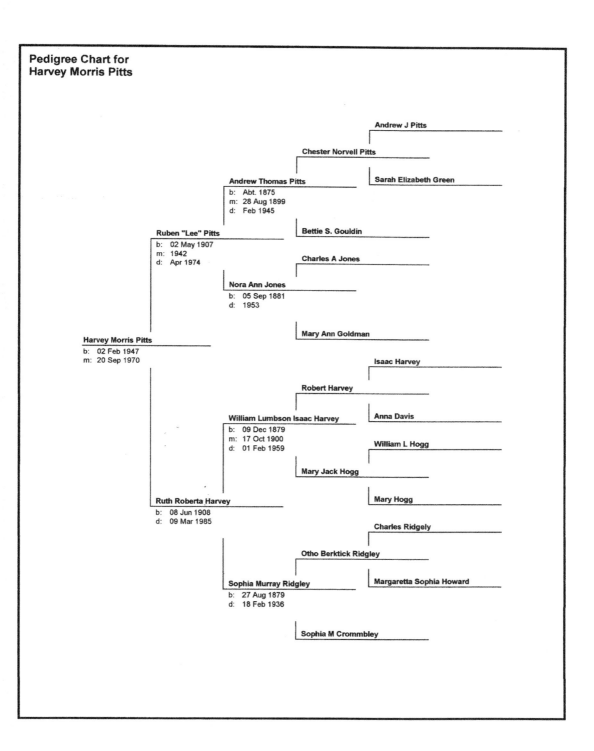

Pedigree Chart for Harvey Morris Pitts

- Harvey Morris Pitts
  - b: 02 Feb 1947
  - m: 20 Sep 1970

- Ruben "Lee" Pitts
  - b: 02 May 1907
  - m: 1942
  - d: Apr 1974

- Andrew Thomas Pitts
  - b: Abt. 1875
  - m: 28 Aug 1899
  - d: Feb 1945

- Chester Norvell Pitts

- Andrew J Pitts

- Sarah Elizabeth Green

- Bettie S. Gouldin

- Nora Ann Jones
  - b: 05 Sep 1881
  - d: 1953

- Charles A Jones

- Mary Ann Goldman

- Ruth Roberta Harvey
  - b: 08 Jun 1908
  - d: 09 Mar 1985

- William Lumbson Isaac Harvey
  - b: 09 Dec 1879
  - m: 17 Oct 1900
  - d: 01 Feb 1959

- Robert Harvey

- Isaac Harvey

- Anna Davis

- Mary Jack Hogg

- William L Hogg

- Mary Hogg

- Sophia Murray Ridgley
  - b: 27 Aug 1879
  - d: 18 Feb 1936

- Otho Berktick Ridgley

- Charles Ridgely

- Margaretta Sophia Howard

- Sophia M Crommbley

MY FAMILY TREE

Paternal Grandfather
Andrew Thomas Pitts
1875–1942

Paternal Grandmother
Nora Ann Jones
1882–1953

Children

Spouses

Mary R. Pitts
1902–

Sprague

Ceylon (Ted) Pitts
1904–1979

Lottie Atkins
1902–1998

Eight children: Junior, Doris, Mildred, Mary Esther, Frances, Hilda, Gaynell, and Paul David

Ruben Lee Pitts (my father)
5/1/1907–4/1/1974

Frances
Ruth Roberta Harvey (my mother)
6/8/1908–3/9/1985
Idonya

Three children from first marriage: Frances, Charles, and ?
Three children from second marriage: Jackie, Harvey, and Donny (my siblings)
Three children from third marriage: Jackie, Gail, and Tim

Beulah Pitts   Jim
1912–2009   Rudy
                                      Arnel (1916–1990)
Two children from first marriage: Jimmy and Philip
One child from second marriage: Patsy
Six children from third marriage: Edward, Warren, Overton, Alease, Margie, and June

John Perry Pitts   Sophia
1915–1977   1908–2004
Two children: Tony and Jimmy

Camel Pitts
1918–

George H. (Andrew) Pitts   Eleanor
1919–   Mabel

Nellie (Joan) Pitts   Ed Thompson
4/13/1921–1/18/2006   5/7/1927–3/30/1995
Eight children: Linda, Teresa, Edward, Robert, Jean, Norann, William, and John

Norma Pitts   Ferris Perks
1924–1952
Two children: Kenny and Ferris

Halorie (Holly) W. Pitts
1926–1959

Maternal Great-grandparents
Robert Harvey
Mary Jack Hogg

Maternal Great-grandparents
Otho Berktick Ridgely
Sophia M. Crommbley

Maternal Grandfather
William Lumbson Harvey
12/9/1879–2/1/1959

Maternal Grandmother
Sophia Murray Ridgely
8/27/1879–2/18/1936

Children

Spouses

Sophia Ridgely Harvey
1902–1/29/1967
Two children: Doris and Jacqueline

Leroy R. Margerum

Robert Bruce Harvey
12/30/1904–3/9/1974
One child: Robert

Jane Marie Spadola
1905–1985

Ruth Roberta Harvey
6/8/1908–3/9/1985

Robert Walter Hansell
Ruben Lee Pitts

Eight children from first marriage: Sophia, Marion, William, Robert, Stanley, Walter, Roberta, Ted
Three children from second marriage: Jackie, Harvey, and Donny

Mary Jack Harvey
8/28/1912–11/8/2000
Two children: Raymond Jr. and Patsy

Raymond Garrett
1909-1971

MORNING CLUB MEMBERS

I SAY GOOD MORNING TO these people and pets who have died, every morning. I'm of the belief that they're not gone until you stop speaking their name. As of 12/21/14 there are currently over 525 names.

Mom, Don, Ted, Betty, Bill, Elaine, Walt, Pat, Eleanor, Eleanor Ann, John, Aunt Jane, Uncle Bob, Bobby, Spock, Serge, Snoopy, Joey, Nellie, Vinny, Louie, Louie, Camille, Duke, Jimmy, Ray, Mike, Maggie, Picarelli, Paula, Anna, Carmela, Andy, Tony, Shorty, Vaa, Colette, Tony, Betty, Cookie, Dolores, Bob, Josephine, Irene, Liz, Dan, Bob, George, Woody, Eileen, Walter McCall, Aunt Agnes, Uncle Phil, Joe, Shirley Futch, Cet, Pop, Grandpop, Milt, Jay, Johnny, Louise, Julia, Pop Messenger, Wade, Art, Terry, Pat, John, Cliff, Bob, Jenny, Carol, Tess, Aunt Mary, Joe, Elaine, Chris, Arlene, Tommy, Deborah, Claudette, Marie, Ginger, Levi, John, Bob, Charlie, Palmer, John, Pearl, Myrtle, Ann, Joe, Doug, Jim, Babette, Howard, Vince, Barbara, Nick, Archie, Keith, Louie, Virginia, John, Ed, Mickie, James, Barney, Cornelius, Juan, Army, Arthur, Charlie, Jean, Jeanie, Mitch, Mike, Carmela, Branford, Gipper, Lillian, Billy, Charlie, Charlie, Elma, Jay, Debbie, Mary, Jim, Jay, Eddie, Addie, Gloria, Larry, Elsie, Phil, Philip, Rose, Sarah, Betty, Earl, Laura, Wheezy, TT, Johnny, Mr. and Mrs. Varano, Tony, Marge, Bud, Mary, Joe, Monique, Monica, Chris, Mike, Herb, Joan, Brandy, Edna, Shirley, Stella, Steve, Dennis, Danny, Velma, Margaret, Fanny, Barbara, Richard Nixon, Jackie Kennedy, Jack and Ted Kennedy, Dominic Quinn, Frank Sinatra, Dean Martin, Ronald Reagan, Margaret Thatcher, Betty and Jerry Ford, Pavarotti, Charlton Heston, Paul Newman, George Carlin, Levi Stubbs, Paul Harvey, Ron Silver, Ed and Johnny, Irv, Farrah, Michael, Liz, Whitney, Dick Clark, Joan Rivers, Annette, Ava, Carmela,

Dave, Carl, Jim, Pat, The Fish, Bunky, Bunky, Mel, The Mom, Whitey, Goldie, Sonny, Chickie, Birdie, Bunny, Birdie, Meadowlark, Rocky, Birdie, Chickie, The Elephant, The 27, Laura, Jerry, Chad, Mrs. Bagot, Mrs. Clark, Jeff, Marvin, Ann, Bert, Bob Nelson, Patsy, Aunt Mary, Aunt Sophia, Tony, Aunt Joan, Uncle Ed, Linda, Aunt Beulah, Hoppy, Nell, Diana, Helen, Snook, Philip, Helen, Kelly, Gia, Jack, Steve, Uncle John, Thelma, Eva, Gary, Josephine, Doris, Bill Foster, Roslyn, Bill, Father Laforge, Ann, Betty, Kimy, Joey, Bernard, Ron, Jim Corey, Greg, Mike, Dan, Joe, Ken, Jimmy, Bill Ridgeway, Walter, Bobby, Josette, Alice, Tony, Nick, Al, Marge, Jimmy, Roman, Bob Benton, Elmer, Chris, Jeff, Lill, Sandy, Florentino, Ellen, Eileen, Beverly, Jackie, Walter, Butch, Trish, Reggie, Herman, Eli, Sister Peg, Mrs. Wells, Palmer Senior, Dawn, Woody, Emma, Fuzzy, Teresa, Sister Romaine, Sister Celeste, Jim, John, Shane, Ed, Janet, Nancy, Francis, Mary, Mike, Joe, Betty, Bonnie, Lucy, Irma, Vinny, Michelle, Francesco, Sal, Louie, Bob, James, Sybil, Chase, Brian, Billy, Franny, Matt, Nancy, Carol, Harry, Midge, Ed, Sue, Cash, Walter, Andy, Millie, Anna, Jimmy, Ruthann, April, John Paul, Father Miller, George, Liz, Richard, Elsie, Kelly, Ray, Helen, Naomi, Stephen, Eileen, Sophia, Andrew, Rocco, Louise, Ed, Danny, Margie, Bill, Jean, Stephen, Ann, Teresa, Frank, Frank, Jules, Jack, Eileen, Herbert, Fred, Frank, Nelda, Virginia, Andy, Allen, Laura, Lina, Rose, Gordon, Vijay, Veloso, Donnie, Chris, Joey, Eileen, Gloria, Eric, Eileen, Fuzzy, Nelda, Gary, Roy, Chris, Elva, Martha, Jimmy, Ed, Walt, Gail, Parkey, Keith, Jimmy, Charlene, Marie, Betty, Adrian, Arlene, Agnes, Edward, Catherine, Frank, Jen, Janet, Evelyn, Ruth, Sam, Sam, Tammy, Tony, Ted, Frank, Jerry, Jack, Al, Dave, Jim, Phil, Leo, Clarence, Patsy, Mike, Keith, Jim, DD, Tim, Albert, Margaret, Bill, Billy, Chris, Chris, Dan, Ed, Gill, Melissa, Judy, Joe, Joe, John, Jim, Jim, Jim, Mark, Roe, Sandy, George, Warren, Hazel, Eleanor, Edith, John Adler, Hal, Roxanne, Ron, Bob, Israel, Shelley, Joe the Roofer, Devon, Chuck, Pete, Mike, Mike, Phil, Frank, Pete, Mary, Mike, Yvonne, Phil, Tom, Dan, Reverend Dan, Rick, Francis, Nace, Norman, Ranger, Oscar, Durand, Sam, Jake, Cayenne, Baron, Taylor, Daisy, Chiclet, Maggie, Heidi, Holly, Apache, Chaps, Simon, Bart, Sam, Max, Dolly, Rosie, Louie, Mr. Big, Wolfee, Max, Weiser, Mr. Spock, Slickie, LT, Squirrelo, Spock, Reds, Freddie, and Jack Newberg.

CPSIA information can be obtained at www.ICGtesting.com
Printed in the USA
BVOW07*0612250915

419590BV00001B/1/P